Have Your Say ①

Have Your Say

Listening and Speaking Skills and Practice

Irene S. McKay

George Brown College

OXFORD
UNIVERSITY PRESS

OXFORD
UNIVERSITY PRESS

Oxford University Press is a department of the University of Oxford.
It furthers the University's objective of excellence in research, scholarship,
and education by publishing worldwide. Oxford is a registered trade mark of
Oxford University Press in the UK and in certain other countries.

Published in Canada by
Oxford University Press
8 Sampson Mews, Suite 204,
Don Mills, Ontario M3C 0H5 Canada

www.oupcanada.com

Copyright © Oxford University Press Canada 2015

The moral rights of the author have been asserted

Database right Oxford University Press (maker)

Library and Archives Canada Cataloguing in Publication
McKay, Irene, author
Have your say 1 : listening and speaking skills and practice / Irene S. McKay.

Accompanied by an audio CD.
ISBN 978-0-19-901169-8 (pbk.).—ISBN 978-0-19-901170-4 (CD)

1. English language—Textbooks for second language learners.   2. English
language—Study and teaching (Higher)—Foreign speakers.   3. English language—
Spoken English—Problems, exercises, etc   I. Title.

PE1128.M1983 2015   428.3'4   C2014-903680-9

Cover image: © Johnny Greig/iStock

Oxford University Press is committed to our environment.
This book is printed on Forest Stewardship Council® certified paper
and comes from responsible sources.

MIX
Paper from
responsible sources
FSC® C004071

Printed and bound in Canada

2   3   4 — 18   17   16

DEDICATION

For Samuel, John, Jocelyn, Ryan and Cassie, who have
brought love and laughter into my life.

AUTHOR ACKNOWLEDGEMENTS

I would like to thank all the ESL/EFL students I have taught, both at George
Brown College and in other contexts. Their struggles and successes in language
learning have provided me with insight and inspiration. I am also indebted to
the many ESL/EFL teachers I have trained. The amazing classroom experiences
I have had enabled me to produce this book. Working with and learning from
dedicated and conscientious learners has motivated me to produce materials
which I believe address learner needs and interests.

I also want to express my gratitude to all my friends and colleagues in ESL and EFL
for continuing to make the field of language teaching so stimulating and exciting.

I am deeply grateful to George Brown College for providing a fertile and
motivating environment for my work.

REVIEWERS

Oxford University Press Canada would like to express appreciation to the
instructors and coordinators who graciously offered feedback on *Have Your
Say 1* at various stages of the developmental process. Their feedback was
instrumental in helping to shape and refine the series.

Patricia Birch	Brandon University	Diane Mensch	Queen's School of English
Jessie Brown	Camosun College	Jane Merivale	Centennial College (formerly)
Lynne Bytyqi	University of Saskatchewan	Patrice Palmer	Mohawk College
Margaret Chell	Université de Montreal Gregory	James Papple	Brock University
		Carolyn Petersen	University of Saskatchewan
Shelagh Cox	Mount Royal University	Jeanne Robinson	Delview Adult Learning Centre (volunteer)
Joan Dundas	Brock University		
John Iveson	Sheridan College	Emily Rosales	Université de Québec à Montréal
Julian L'Enfant	Saint Mary's University TESL Centre		
		Mary Tang	Centennial College
Angela Losito	Université de Sherbrooke	Tony Vernon	Camosun College

Scope and Sequence Chart

CHAPTER	LISTENING Selections	SPEAKING		
		Communication Focus	Grammar Skills	PRONUNCIATION
1 **GETTING TO KNOW YOU—** Introductions and Descriptions	(1A) Meeting People: Introductions (1B) Describing People: A Conversation (2) Making a Good First Impression: An Interview	Making introductions Greeting Describing Comparing	• Verb *to be*: present tense • Adjectives • Prepositions of place: *in, at* • Verb *to be*: past tense • Comparatives	• Reduced forms of pronouns • Contractions— pronouns and the verb *to be* • Number of Syllables • Pronunciation contrast: /ʌ/ as in *but*, /ʊ/ as in *good*, and /uw/ as in *true*
2 **ALL IN A DAY'S WORK—** Routines, Habits, and Occupations	(1) Routines and Schedules: A Conversation (2) A Day in the Life: A Special Report	Describing habits and routines Checking understanding and asking for clarification Stating reasons	• Simple present tense • Adverbs of frequency • Telling time • Subordinate conjunction: *because*	• Pronunciation of regular plurals • Pronunciation of the third-person singular of the simple present tense • Number of Syllables • Pronunciation contrast: /w/ and /v/
3 **EASY COME, EASY GO—** Shopping, Money, and Numbers	(1) The Best Way to Shop: A Conversation (2) The History of Money: A Short Lecture	Giving information about actions in progress Expressing ability and inability Expressing ability in the past Making requests for permission	• Present progressive tense • Modals: *can/can't*— ability • Modals: *could/ couldn't*—past ability • Modals: *may/can/ could*—requests for permission • Cardinal and ordinal numbers	• Pronunciation contrast: *can* and *can't* • Pronunciation contrast: /iy/ and /ɪ/ • Pronunciation of numbers • Pronunciation contrast: /l/ and /r/
4 **LET ME ENTERTAIN YOU—** Leisure Activities, Interests, and Hobbies	(1) Famous Celebrities: A Conversation (2) How to Study For Tests: An Information Session	Expressing likes and dislikes Starting and closing conversations Giving instructions Making general requests	• Verbs followed by nouns and gerunds • Verbs followed by infinitives • Verbs followed by objects and infinitives • Sequential markers—*first, second, next, after that, then, finally*	• Pronunciation of unstressed vowels (schwa) • Rising intonation

CHAPTER	LISTENING Selections	SPEAKING		PRONUNCIATION
		Communication Focus	Grammar Skills	
⑤ YOU ARE WHAT YOU EAT— Food and Experiences	(1) Food and Eating Habits in Other Countries: An Interview (2) Making Excuses: Conversations	Talking about completed actions Telling a story about the past Making excuses and giving explanations Talking about actions in progress at specific times in the past	• Count and mass nouns • Past tense of regular and irregular verbs • Past progressive tense	• Pronunciation of regular past tense endings • Consonant clusters at the beginnings and ends of words
⑥ LET THE GOOD TIMES ROLL— Holidays and Special Celebrations	(1) New Year's Celebrations around the World: A Report (2) "The Gift of a Goat": CBC News Report	Expressing future plans and intentions Talking about seasons and the weather Making predictions Stating plans, arrangements, and intentions Inviting people to do activities	• *to be going to—* future • Modal: *will*—future • Present progressive tense	• Reduced form: *gonna* • Pronunciation contrast: /a/ and /ow/ • Falling intonation
⑦ KEEPING IN SHAPE— Health and Fitness	(1) Siblings: A Conversation (2) Parasports: CBC News Report	Asking for and giving advice Expressing necessity Making suggestions Expressing necessity in the past	• Modals: *should/ shouldn't—* advisability • Modals: *must/ have to*: necessity, present and past	• Pronunciation of consonant sound /θ/ • Pronunciation of consonant sound /ð/ • Pronunciation contrast: consonants /ʃ/, /tʃ/, /dʒ/, and /ʒ/
⑧ DISCOVERING OUR WONDERFUL WORLD— Travel and Experiences	(1) Travel Stories: CBC Radio Interview (2) Space Travel: CBC News Report	Talking about experiences and achievements Talking about actions begun in the past and continuing into the present Describing and comparing	• Present perfect tense • Present perfect progressive tense • Superlatives	• Pronunciation contrast: vowels /a/ and /æ/ • Pronunciation contrast: vowels /ey/ and /ɛ/

Contents

CHAPTER 2

CHAPTER 3

CHAPTER 4

LET ME ENTERTAIN YOU—Leisure Activities, Interests, and Hobbies   88

CHAPTER 5

YOU ARE WHAT YOU EAT—Food and Experiences   113

CHAPTER 6

LET THE GOOD TIMES ROLL—Holidays and Special Celebrations   145

CHAPTER 7

KEEPING IN SHAPE—Health and Fitness   173

CHAPTER 8

DISCOVERING OUR WONDERFUL WORLD—Travel and Experiences   203

INTRODUCTION

Overview

Audience

Have Your Say 1 is a listening and speaking skills and practice text for high beginners in Intensive English, English for Academic Purposes, LINC, and other ESL programs. It is designed to take learners from Benchmark 3 to Benchmark 5 of the Canadian Language Benchmarks. It is the first book in a three-level course in listening and speaking.

Approach

Have Your Say 1 incorporates some of the popular features of the previous *Have Your Say* text such as pronunciation and vocabulary. It is based on the concept that learner-centredness and exposure to authentic, meaningful language in collaborative activities motivate learners and provide them with the means for developing proficiency in listening and speaking. As learners communicate orally, their confidence in their abilities to communicate increases, and this eventually leads to improved listening and speaking skills. The text provides scaffolding and activities to enable learners to expand their communicative competence.

Have Your Say listening and speaking activities provide the learners with meaningful tasks that give them a real reason to communicate verbally in English. There is a focus on both form and function. Learners are motivated to talk and share their experiences and feelings. The materials are constructed so that they can be a jumping-off point for further conversations. An important feature of the materials is that they help to foster an accepting atmosphere in the language classroom which makes learners feel secure, valued, and free to experiment with the language in expressing themselves. The activities provide variety in topics, groupings, language skills addressed, and task types to keep the learners engaged.

Features of the Text

Listening Sections

Each chapter contains two main listening sections. The content of each of the listening texts is related to the overall theme of the chapter. There is variety in the types of listening. Some are conversations of relevance to beginning-level learners. Others are short lectures, reports, and interviews, which prepare learners for longer listening texts. Since the goal of all listening activities is to prepare learners to eventually comprehend authentic listening materials, several selections are authentic radio or TV programs chosen for their comprehensibility and length to make them accessible to lower-level learners. It's important for English language learners to be exposed to authentic language, even at the lower levels.

Pre-listening Activities

Each main listening section is introduced by pre-listening activities. Some of these encourage top-down processing, which occurs when learners exploit their background knowledge to understand texts. These include speaking exercises; the use of pictures, quizzes, surveys; and other activities to engage the learners in thinking and talking about the topic and in this way to activate their background knowledge. Each listening section also contains activities to encourage bottom-up processing, which occurs when learners use their grammatical and lexical knowledge to aid comprehension. These include exercises focusing on the vocabulary used in the recording.

During-Listening Activities

There are two main kinds of during-listening activities: Listening for the Main Ideas asks the learners to understand the overall gist of the text, and Listening Comprehension requires the learners to listen for specific information in the text. Each listening selection has both types of activities.

Personalizing

The final activity for each listening selection is Personalizing, which engages the learners in analyzing or evaluating the information they heard and reacting to it.

Speaking Sections

Almost all ESL/EFL learners complain that they do not get enough speaking practice. *Have Your Say 1* provides a wide variety of speaking activities to involve learners as much as possible in using language meaningfully. Each chapter contains two main speaking sections, each of which includes a number of Communication Focuses. Speaking activities occur before and after the listening sections and impress upon learners the importance of oral communication skills.

Communication Focus

Each Speaking section begins with a Communication Focus; others occur as needed. The purpose of each Communication Focus is to introduce speech acts and language functions. They focus the learners' attention on certain language functions and encourage them to produce these during the speaking activities.

Speaking Activities

The speaking activities are linked to the theme of the chapter. They are related to and support the Communication Focus sections. Speaking activities appear in both the Listening and the Speaking sections. The speaking activities include interviews and questionnaires in which there is an information gap, partner and group activities in which the learners collaborate to reach a goal, short group and individual presentations, whole-class activities, communication games, and role plays. These activities are designed to encourage learners to produce a large quantity of language, which will eventually lead to improved speaking skills.

Grammar Notes

The Speaking sections often include one or more summaries of the grammatical structures the learners are encouraged to use during the chapter's speaking activities. The aim of the Grammar Notes is to encourage students to produce these structures at the same time as they are working on improving their fluency.

Listening and Speaking Strategies

Where relevant, various specific strategies primarily for developing listening and speaking skills appear in the margins throughout the chapters. Teachers can use these as jumping-off points both to discuss the strategies learners can use and to encourage learners to try to use new strategies to progress in their everyday communication.

Pronunciation Sections

Each chapter contains one or more pronunciation focuses—these may deal with segmentals (individual sounds) or suprasegmentals (features greater than individual sounds such as intonation). The pronunciation activities involve distinguishing and identifying a particular aspect of English pronunciation and then producing it. Learners are asked to practise pronunciation with each other in a variety of activities.

Communicating in the Real World

Each chapter contains a final section which asks the learners to take what they have learned and apply it beyond the classroom. Learners are asked to speak to people who are not in their classes, asking some of the questions they have been discussing in the chapter, and to then present their findings and experiences to the class. In some chapters, students can also work on projects and presentations which take them outside the classroom to extend their learning.

Self-Evaluation

When learners take responsibility for their learning, both language proficiency and strategy use increase. Each chapter ends with a self-evaluation section which allows learners to reflect on what they have accomplished and to consider where they need to improve and what they still need to learn. Students can complete these evaluations individually, or the sections can be used as the basis for journal writing or discussion.

CHAPTER 1

Getting to Know You

Introductions and Descriptions

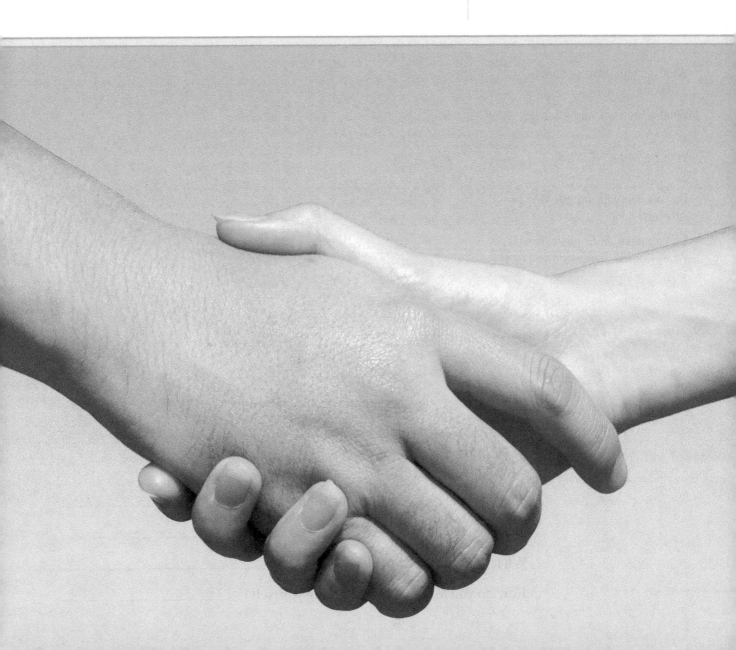

You're going to call me WHAT??

THINKING AND TALKING

Discuss these questions with a partner.

Why is this baby worried?

Why are names important?

👥 SPEAKING ACTIVITY 1

Answer these questions and then ask your partner. Tell the class about your partner.

Questions	Me	My Partner
What's your first name?		
What's your family name or surname?		
What do you want people to call you?		
What does your name mean?		
Who named you? Why?		
Do you like your name? Why or why not?		
Do you have an English name? What English names do you like?		
A famous movie star named her baby "Apple." Is that a good name? Can a mother or father give their baby any name they want? Explain.		

LISTENING 1A

Before You Listen

When was the last time you introduced yourself? _____

What did you say? _____

What did the other people say? _____

How do you feel about introducing yourself? _____

Listening for the Main Ideas

Listen to each conversation and circle the place where the conversation takes place.

 Track 1

- in a business office
- at a party
- in an apartment building
- in an evening class
- on the bus

- on the telephone
- in a French class
- in a restaurant
- in a doctor's office

Listening Comprehension

Listen to the conversations as many times as necessary and fill in the chart about each conversation.

Track 2

Conversation 1		
Names	Man's first name	Woman's first name
	Tom	Lucy
Other Information	They are neighbours. They live in the same building.	

Conversation 2				
Names	Man's first name	Man's last name	Woman's first name	Woman's last name
Other Information				

Conversation 3				
Names	Man's first name	Man's last name	Woman's first name	Woman's last name
Other Information				

Conversation 4						
Names	Instructor's first name	Instructor's last name	Man's first name	Man's last name	Woman's first name	Woman's last name
Other Information						

Personalizing

Work with a partner and talk about how people introduce themselves in other countries. Talk about some things that are the same and some things that are different. Report to the class.

What is the same in other countries?

1. _____
2. _____

What is different?

1. _____
2. _____

SPEAKING 1

Communication Focus 1:
Making Introductions: Introducing Yourself

Introductions	Examples	Responses
Hello, I'm. . .	Hello, I'm Jason	Hi, Jason. I'm Marie.
Hi, my name is. . .	Hi, my name is Ellen.	Hi, Ellen. My name is Nelly.
I'd like to introduce myself. I'm. . .	I'd like to introduce myself. I'm Ian.	Hi, Ian. It's nice to meet you. Hello, Ian. I'm glad to meet you. Hello, Ian. Pleased to meet you. [This is more formal.]

SPEAKING ACTIVITY 2

As a whole class, line up in alphabetical order according to your first name. For example, Alex will be before Barbara and Barbara will come before Cathy, and so on. Once the lineup is complete, each person will introduce himself/herself and all the other people before him/her. For example, Alex will say, "Hello, I'd like to introduce myself, I'm Alex." Barbara will say, "Hello, I'd like to introduce myself, I'm Barbara and this is Alex." Cathy will say, "Hello I'd like to introduce myself, I'm Cathy and this is Barbara and that is Alex." Continue until everyone in the class introduces himself/herself and all the other students before them.

Speaking STRATEGY

If you can use expressions for introducing, greeting, and saying goodbye, English conversations will be easier for you.

👤👤👤 SPEAKING ACTIVITY 3

Work in groups of three. Put the expressions of greeting and saying goodbye in the correct places on the chart below. Add other expressions that you know.

Hello.	Good day.	Good evening.
See you later.	What's up?	How's it going?
Hi!	Bye now.	Keep in touch.
So long.	Have a good one.	Good afternoon.
Hey!	Take care.	Good night.
Long time, no see!	How are things going?	

Greetings	Saying Goodbye

👤👤 SPEAKING ACTIVITY 4

What body language do people use when they greet each other in your home country? Circle the correct actions and explain these to your partner. Your partner will report to the class.

bow

handshake

look at the floor during introductions

hug

kiss

pat on arm or back

take off hat

other _____

👥 SPEAKING ACTIVITY 5

A nickname is a short name that people use if they think that their full name is too long or too formal. Work with a partner and use the list below to fill in the nicknames next to the full names on the chart.

Bill	Ted	Larry	Tony	Nick	Jim	Bernie
Beth	Dick	Joe	Debbie	Jan	Bob	Chuck
Mandy	Cindy	Cathy	Andy	Dan	Hank	Pat

Full Name	Nickname	Full Name	Nickname
William	Bill	Elizabeth	
Robert		Janice	
Andrew		James	
Patricia		Anthony	
Amanda		Deborah	
Cynthia		Lawrence	
Catherine		Nicolas	
Bernard		Theodore	
Charles		Richard	
Daniel		Joseph	
Henry			

👤👤👤 SPEAKING ACTIVITY 6

Make a quick chart with the headings shown below. Work in groups of five. Introduce yourself. Fill in the chart. Report about the students in your group.

First Name	Last Name	Nickname

Communication Focus 2:
Making Introductions: Introducing Others

Structures/Expressions	Examples	Responses
This is . . .	This is Erika.	It's nice to meet you, Erika.
I want you to meet. . .	I want you to meet Emily.	I'm glad to meet you, Emily.
I'd like to introduce. . .	I'd like to introduce David.	I'm pleased to meet you, David.

👥 SPEAKING ACTIVITY 7

Work in groups of three. Write out the questions. Then find out the information from your partners. Then join another group and take turns introducing each other.

Questions	Partner 1	Partner 2
First name: Q.: *What's your first name?*		
Nickname:		
Nationality:		
Occupation:		
Hobby:		

Grammar Note: The Verb *to be*

The verb *to be* is the most irregular verb in English. We use the verb *to be* to state a name, a place or location, a time or date, or a description.

Examples:

I am Stephanie.   Toronto is interesting.

I am in Toronto.   I am happy.

It is Monday.

These are the forms of the verb *to be*.

Affirmative	Contractions	Examples
I am	I'm	I'm tired.
you are	you're	You're happy.
we are	we're	We're sad.
they are	they're	They're funny.
she is	she's	She's quiet.
he is	he's	He's noisy.
it is	it's	It's cold.

continued on next page

Negative	Contractions	Examples
I am not	I'm not	I'm not tired.
you are not	you aren't	You aren't happy.
we are not	we aren't	We aren't sad.
they are not	they aren't	They aren't funny.
she is not	she isn't	She isn't quiet.
he is not	he isn't	He isn't noisy.
it is not	it isn't	It isn't cold.

Verb *to be*	Interrogative Forms
am I	Am I late?
are you	Are you hungry?
are we	Are we right?
are they	Are they wrong?
is she	Is she absent?
is he	Is he sick?
is it	Is it easy?

SPEAKING ACTIVITY 8

Make sentences and then share your sentences with a partner. Report your answers to the class.

Speaking STRATEGY

When you don't understand, ask the speaker to repeat. Ask as often as necessary.

Here are some expressions to use:

- I beg your pardon?
- Pardon me?
- Pardon?
- Please repeat that.
- Please speak more slowly.

1. Make two affirmative statements about yourself.
   a. _____
   b. _____

2. Make two negative statements about your teacher.
   a. _____
   b. _____

3. Make two statements about your classmates.
   a. _____
   b. _____

4. Make two questions about people in your class.
   a. _____
   b. _____

SPEAKING ACTIVITY 9

A. Make a quick chart with headings shown on the next page. Walk around the room and talk to as many students as possible. Find out the answers to these questions and report to the class.

Name	What is your favourite season?	What is your favourite day of the week?	What is your favourite food?	What is your favourite drink?	What is your favourite colour?

B. Write about two classmates you talked to.

Communication Focus 3: Describing

We use adjectives to describe nouns such as people, things, and places.
Examples:

> Toronto is a <u>new</u> city. Mexico City is an <u>old</u> city.

> I have a <u>new blue</u> jacket.

> My cat is <u>afraid</u> of <u>loud</u> noises.

Most adjectives in English come before the noun.*

Adjectives can be in the subject or in the predicate of the sentence.

Adjectives do not change their form for singular or plural.
Examples:

> The <u>old</u> car is outside.   The car is very <u>old</u>.

*A very small number of adjectives cannot come before the noun. Some of these are *afraid, alone, awake, asleep.*
Examples:

> The student is afraid. NOT: The afraid student

> The children are alone. NOT: The alone children

👥 SPEAKING ACTIVITY 10

Work with a partner. Write new sentences with the opposite of the adjectives in the sentences below. Work fast! The pair who finishes first is the winner.

1. It isn't her last name.   _It's her first name_____.

2. They aren't early.   _____.

3. She isn't happy.   _____.

4. The building isn't low.   _____.

5. This isn't the north side. _____.

6. Her house isn't in the east end. _____.

7. Turtles aren't fast. _____.

8. Soft drinks aren't good for you. _____.

9. We aren't outside. _____.

10. He isn't a rich man. _____.

11. She isn't careful. _____.

12. You aren't lucky. _____.

13. The chair isn't hard. _____.

14. Groceries aren't expensive. _____.

15. The street car isn't fast. _____.

16. This colour isn't bright. _____.

17. The knife isn't dull. _____.

18. Her homework isn't messy. _____.

19. He isn't asleep. _____.

SPEAKING ACTIVITY 11

A. Work with a partner. Write the opposite of each adjective in the list. Then put a check mark next to the adjectives that we use for people. After that, circle the adjectives that describe you and put a square around those that describe your partner.

Adjective	Opposite	Adjective	Opposite
attractive		shy	
tall		intelligent	
fat		dangerous	
heavy		strong	
quiet		beautiful	
pretty		straight	
handsome		clever	
interesting		new	
talkative		high	
slim		relaxed	
long		brave	
easy		healthy	
skinny		sweet	
funny		expensive	
cold		dry	
old			

B. By yourself, use three adjectives to describe yourself and three adjectives to describe your partner. Compare your sentences with your partner. Tell the class about the differences.

Me

1. _____
2. _____
3. _____

My partner

1. _____
2. _____
3. _____

SPEAKING ACTIVITY 12

Circle the adjectives in the list below that describe your hair and eyes. Then write a sentence to describe you and one to describe your partner. Tell the class about your partner.

Examples:

> I am a tall, thin, shy woman with short curly brown hair and blue eyes. My partner is a friendly young woman with long black hair and brown eyes.

curly	straight	short	long	thick	blue	wavy
green	red	black	blonde	grey	brown	

Me

_____

My partner

_____

LISTENING 1B

Before You Listen

Work with a partner and describe the colours and patterns in the clothing. What are your favourite colours and patterns?

  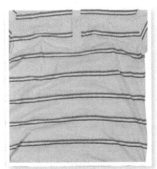 

PRE-LISTENING VOCABULARY

A. You will hear a conversation on the audio CD that includes the following words. Work with a partner or by yourself to find the definition of each word. Write the word beside its definition.

chubby   bald   moustache   height   suit   skinny

interview   plaid   striped   cheerful   outgoing   bright   polka dot

Definitions	Vocabulary
1. a checked pattern	plaid
2. intelligent and upbeat	
3. material with a pattern of lines or bands on it	
4. material with a pattern of regular dots on it	
5. happy	
6. not having any hair on the head	
7. how tall a person is	
8. friendly and able to talk easily with others	
9. hair on the face, growing between the nose and the lips	
10. a short meeting for a special reason, such as a job	
11. very thin	
12. jacket and pants or skirt of the same material	
13. heavy in weight; fat	

B. Choose the correct vocabulary words from the list to fill in the blanks in these sentences. Use each word only once. Not all the words are used in the sentences.

1. She isn't a sad person. She's very _____ cheerful _____.

2. He has a _____ because he doesn't like to shave.

3. Everyone likes him because he's a _____ young man.

4. She is not a shy person. She's very _____.

5. _____ men aren't as handsome as men with hair.

6. Those children are _____ because they don't eat very much.

7. It's a good idea to wear a _____ to a job interview.

8. Small babies are usually _____.

ii PRE-LISTENING ACTIVITY

Look at the list below. Circle the words for the clothes that you have on. Circle the words for the colours of your clothes. Write one sentence to describe yourself and one sentence to describe your partner. Compare your sentences.

Example:

> I am a tall, thin, shy woman with a black T-shirt, green pants, and a black jacket.

pants	jacket	dress	running shoes	T-shirt	socks
blouse	shorts	hoodie	skirt	sweater	shirt
tights	jeans	suit	dress	coat	cap
yellow	orange	green	blue	red	purple
pink	black	grey	white	brown	beige

Me

_____

My partner

_____

Listening for the Main Ideas

Listen to the conversation and answer the questions.

🎧 Track 3

1. What are the man and the woman talking about?

2. Where are they?

3. Why are talking about this?

Listening Comprehension

Listen to the conversation as many times as necessary and fill in the missing information for each of the people, as in the example.

🎧 Track 4

Mary Ann Thomas

Hair: long straight blonde _____

Height: short _____

Weight: chubby _____

Clothes: jean jacket, black skirt _____

Personality: quiet and shy _____

Listening STRATEGY 👂

Try to listen for specific information. This helps you understand the listening.

Fred Jones

Hair: _____

Height: _____

Weight: _____

Clothes: _____

Personality: _____

Terry Williams

Hair: _____

Height: _____

Weight: _____

Clothes: _____

Personality: _____

Ellen Simpson

Hair: _____

Height: _____

Weight: _____

Clothes: _____

Personality: _____

Alison McDonald

Hair: _____

Height: _____

Weight: _____

Clothes: _____

Personality: _____

Bruce Thompson

Hair: _____

Height: _____

Weight: _____

Clothes: _____

Personality: _____

Personalizing

A. Work in groups of three. Discuss how you want people to describe you.

Description	Me	Partner 1	Partner 2
Hair			
Height			
Weight			
Personality			
Other			

B. As a group, decide which adjectives people in North America don't like to use because they are negative. Circle them.

fat   plump   old   ugly   skinny   slim

talkative   ordinary   noisy   messy   heavy   boring

stupid   smart   funny

Vocabulary and Language Chunks

Write the number of the expression next to the meaning. After checking your answers choose five expressions and write your own sentences.

Words and Expressions	Meaning
1. who's who	_____ to appear interesting
2. to have on	_____ hair which is not straight, not curly, with waves in it
3. medium height	_____ a place where people wait
4. wavy hair	_____ a soft hat with a visor
5. waiting area	_____ a jacket made of denim material
6. baseball cap	_____ not tall and not short
7. jean jacket	___1___ telling which person is which
8. to look interesting	_____ to wear

ꙮ SPEAKING ACTIVITY 13

This is a game. Work with a partner. Write a description of three people in your class. Write each description on a separate small piece of paper. Write the name of the person on the back of each paper. The teacher will collect the papers in a box. The teacher will divide the class into two teams. The teacher will then take a paper and read the description. The team who is the first to guess the name scores a point. Use questions or statements in your guesses. Use complete sentences. The team with the highest score wins.

Example:

Teacher: <u>Who is the</u> tall, thin student with the black hoodie?

Student from team A: <u>Is the</u> tall, thin student with the black hoodie Alex?

OR

<u>I think</u> Alex <u>is</u> the tall, thin student with the black hoodie.

Grammar Note: Order of Adjectives

If we use two or more adjectives together we need to put them in a certain order. Look at these examples and try to find the rule for the order of adjectives.

a beautiful big blue hat   a tall Chinese student

an expensive red ~~wool~~ *lana* sweater   a long black leather coat

the old red brick house   a new English dictionary

👥 SPEAKING ACTIVITY 14

Work with a partner. Write new sentences using the adjectives. The pair who finishes first and has the largest number of correct answers is the winner.

1. I live in a building. It's yellow. It's small.

    I live in a small yellow building.

2. Eve is a student. She is Japanese. She is smart.

    _____

3. These are my shoes. They are leather. They are red. They are expensive.

    They are my expensive, red, leather shoes

4. Is that your T-shirt? It's cotton. It's new. It's white.

    Is that your new, white, cotton T-shirt?

5. Is this your book? It's English. It's old.

    Is this your old English book?

6. Let's visit the park. It's beautiful. It's big.

    Let's visite the beautiful big park.

7. Look at the children. They are little. They are happy.

    look at the happy little children

8. Is this classroom ours? It's big. It's modern.

   It's big modern classroom

9. Where is your cellphone? It's new. It's expensive.

   it's expensive new cellphone.

10. He has a sweater on. It's wool. It's orange. It's bright.
    brillante

    He has a bright orange wool sweather

Grammar Note: The Verb *to be*—Past Tense

These are the forms of the verb *to be* in the past tense. We use the past
tense with time expressions like these:

last Monday	an hour ago	yesterday
last week	five years ago	before
last year	three months ago	
last June	a while ago	

These are the past forms of the verb *to be*:

Affirmative	Negative	Questions
I was	I wasn't	Was I?
he was	he wasn't	Was he?
she was	she wasn't	Was she?
it was	it wasn't	Was it?
you were	you weren't	Were you?
we were	we weren't	Were we?
they were	they weren't	Were they?

Grammar Note: Prepositions of Place—*in/at*

When we talk about places we use different prepositions. Use *at* for buildings
or places when the meaning is general. Use *in* for cities or countries, or to
mean inside a place. With a few nouns we don't use a preposition.

Examples:

at church	in New York	go downtown
at school	in Toronto	go home
at home	in Vancouver	go outside
at work	in Canada	
at a park	in China	

at a party	in the USA
at home	in the library
at a restaurant	in the supermarket
at the library	
at the movies	

 SPEAKING ACTIVITY 15

Make a quick chart with the headings shown below. Walk around the room and talk to as many classmates as possible. Write the information on your chart. Report to the class about three students. Ask these questions.

Where were you two years ago?

Who were you with?

What were your feelings? Were you happy or sad, tired, relaxed, or something else?

What was the reason?

Name	Location	With Whom	Feelings	Reason

Write about two of your classmates.

 SPEAKING ACTIVITY 16

Work with a partner. Answer these questions and find out the information from your partner. Tell the class the most interesting information about your partner.

Questions	Me	My Partner
Where were you last night?		
Where were you last summer?		
Where were you last Saturday night?		
Where were you last New Year's Eve?		
Where were you on your last vacation?		
Where were you after school yesterday?		

SPEAKING ACTIVITY 17

Make a quick chart with the headings shown below. Walk around the room and talk to as many people as possible. Report to the class about three people.

Ask these questions:	**Possible answers:**
Where were you born?	I was born in China.
What year were you born in?	I was born in 1995.
What month were you born in?	I was born in January.
When were you born?	I was born on January 30.

Name	Where?	What Year?	What Month?	When?

SPEAKING 2

Communication Focus 4: Comparing

We can use adjectives to compare people, things, and places.

Grammar Note: Comparatives 1

When we use adjectives to compare two people or things, we add *-er* to short adjectives of one syllable, and we use *than* to make the comparison.
Examples:

> Mary is shorter than Samantha.

> Samantha is older than Mary.

For adjectives of two syllables ending in *y*, we also add *-er* to form the comparative.
Examples:

> Mary is prettier than Samantha.

> Samantha is friendlier than Mary.

Spelling note: For two-syllable adjectives ending in *y*, change the *y* to *i*.
Example:

> The woman was angrier than the man.

SPEAKING ACTIVITY 18

A. Compare yourself to your classmates. Talk to as many people as possible to complete the chart below.

Example:

tall   Sam is taller than I am.

Find someone who is:

Name	Adjective	Comparison
	tall	
	friendly	
	short	
	heavy	
	light	
	strong	
	weak	
	old	
	young	
	big	
	small	
	thin	
	busy	
	quiet	
	smart	

B. Write about two of your classmates.

SPEAKING ACTIVITY 19

Work with a partner. Compare the following pairs of items. For each, use the adjective in the chart. When you finish, join another group. Compare your answers.

Compare	Adjectives
an apple/a chocolate bar	healthy *An apple is a healthier snack than a chocolate bar.*
a bicycle/a car	safe
an airplane/a ship	fast

Compare	Adjectives
the city/the country	dirty
summer vacation/ Christmas vacation	long
an elephant/a lion	large
a tiger/a monkey	brave
cats/dogs	friendly
roses/daisies	pretty
men/women	strong
a house/an apartment	cheap
reading/writing	easy
a lake/an ocean	deep
a big city/a small town	busy
planes/trains	slow

SPEAKING ACTIVITY 20

A. Look at the list of adjectives. Circle the ones that describe this city. Put a square around those that describe the last city you lived in.

old   friendly   new   pretty   ugly   busy

quiet   safe   big   small   noisy

B. Compare this city to the last city you lived in. Make three comparisons. Then compare your answers with your partner's. Report to the class about some things that are the same as and some things that are different from your partner's comparisons.

1. _____

2. _____

3. _____

Grammar Note: Equatives

When we compare two things or people, and want to show that they are the same in the qualities we are describing, we use the structure *as . . . _____ as. . . .*

Example:

Motorcycles are <u>as fast as</u> cars.

We can also use this structure in the negative.

Examples:

I'm <u>not as tall as</u> my sister.

Toronto <u>isn't as expensive as</u> New York.

🏃 SPEAKING ACTIVITY 21

Work with a partner. Make a comparative statement with the same meaning as each sentence.

Put a check mark next to those statements that you agree with.

1. Country air is cleaner than city air.

   <u>City air isn't as clean as country air.</u>

2. The country is quieter than the city.

   _____

3. City life is busier than country life.

   _____

4. The country is safer than the city.

   _____

5. Prices in the city are higher than prices in the country.

   _____

6. The food in the country is fresher than the food in the city.

   _____

7. Life in the country is slower than life in the city.

   _____

8. People in the country are happier than people in the city.

   _____

9. Life in the country is better than life in the city.

   _____

Grammar Note: Comparatives 2

When we use adjectives of two or more syllables to compare two people
or things, we use *more* and *than* to make the comparison.
Examples:

> Mary is <u>more</u> intelligent <u>than</u> Samantha.

> Samantha is <u>more</u> careful <u>than</u> Mary.

Exceptions: a few adjectives of two syllables can use either *more* or *-er
than* to form the comparative.
Examples:

> He is <u>more handsome than</u> his brother.

> He is <u>handsomer than</u> his brother.

Some other adjectives which can use either *-er* or *more* are *narrow, gentle,
quiet, clever, cruel.*

PRONUNCIATION ACTIVITY 1

A. Listen to these words and write down the number of syllables, then
check your work with a partner and the teacher.

 **Track 5**

Adjective	Number of Syllables	Comparative Form
tall	1	taller than
narrow	2	more narrow than/narrower than
interesting		
good		
small		
weak		
heavy		
bad		
wide		
noisy		
quiet		
cheap		
ugly		
clever		
difficult		
high		
beautiful		
dangerous		

B. Write out the comparative forms. Practise saying the words with
a partner.

👥 SPEAKING ACTIVITY 22

Work in small groups. Discuss each of these questions together. Try to agree on your answers. Report to the class.

1. Which are more intelligent—cats or dogs?
2. Which is more boring—doing the dishes or doing ironing?
3. Which is more interesting—going to the movies or going to a play?
4. Which city is more modern—Toronto or New York?
5. Which country is more beautiful—Canada or the USA?
6. Which activity is more exciting—going to a party or going to an amusement park?
7. Which animal is more dangerous—a tiger or an elephant?
8. Which subject is more difficult—reading or writing?
9. Which is more difficult—studying for a test or writing a paragraph?
10. Which is better—playing a video game by yourself or playing a video game with someone?
11. Which is more expensive—buying books or buying clothes?
12. Who is more careful—men or women?

LISTENING 2

Before You Listen

PRE-LISTENING VOCABULARY

A. You will hear a conversation on the audio CD that includes the following words. Work with a partner or by yourself to write the definition of each word.

guest   expert   impression   tips   occasion   posture

neat   sloppy   opinion   great

Definition	Vocabulary
1. event, activity	*occasion*
2. excellent, very good	
3. a person who knows a lot about something	
4. the way people stand, sit, or hold their bodies	
5. clean, organized, not messy	
6. a person who is invited	
7. a feeling or idea we have the first time we see someone or something	
8. something we believe or think	
9. short pieces of advice or information	
10. messy; not organized; not clean; careless	

B. Choose the correct vocabulary words from the list to fill in the blanks in these sentences. Use each word only once. Not all the words are used in the sentences. Please make changes to the nouns and verbs if necessary.

Listening STRATEGY 🔊
If you think about what you are going to listen to and try to predict some information that you will hear, this will make listening easier.

1. Everybody wants to make a good __impression__ when they meet someone new.

2. A few seconds after we meet a new person we have an idea or _____ about them.

3. When you meet someone for the first time you want to look _____. You don't want to look _____ and careless.

4. Marilyn Adams knows a lot about psychology. She's an _____.

5. Dr. Adams gives people information or _____ about making a good impression.

6. If you have poor _____, you don't look very sure of yourself.

7. When you meet someone for the first time you need to dress the right way for the _____.

8. The host always welcomes the _____.

9. If you prepare for an interview you can make not just a good impression, but a _____ impression.

👥 **PRE-LISTENING ACTIVITY**

1. Work with a partner and describe the people in the picture.

   Where are they?

   What is the situation?

2. Work with a partner. Make a mind map of how to make a good first impression.

How to make a good first impression

3. With your partner predict four things that you think the speakers will say about how to make a good first impression.

a. _____

b. _____

c. _____

d. _____

Listening for the Main Ideas

Track 6   Listen to the interview as many times as necessary and answer the questions.

1. Where are the speakers?

_____

2. Why are they talking about this topic?

_____

Listening Comprehension

Track 7   Listen to the interview as many times as necessary to write the answers to the questions.

1. What's the name of the guest?

Her name is Dr. Marilyn Adams.

2. Why does she say it's important to make a good first impression?

_____

3. How long does it take to get an impression of someone?

_____

4. What does she say a greeting includes?

_____

5. What are five tips she gives?

a. _____

b. _____

c. _____

d. _____

e. _____

6. How many of your predictions were correct?

Personalizing

A. There is a saying in the listening: "You never get a second chance to make a first impression." Do you think this is true? Why?

B. Can a first impression be wrong? Tell your partner about a time your first impression of someone was wrong.

Vocabulary and Language Chunks

Write the number of the expression next to the meaning. After checking your answers, choose five expressions and write your own sentences.

Expressions	**Meanings**
1. to make a good impression	_____ to look at the good, positive things
2. to have an opinion	_____ at the exact time, not late
3. the right way	_____ to look directly at someone
4. on time	_____ normal good judgment
5. to look someone in the eye	_____ do something as well as you can
6. to do your best	_____ to have an idea, belief
7. common sense	_____ in the correct manner
8. the way you look	___1___ to produce a positive, good effect on
9. to look on the bright side	_____ your appearance

PRONUNCIATION

Pronunciation Focus 1:
Reduced Forms of Pronouns and the Verb *to be*

These are the pronouns in English. We do not usually stress or pronounce them strongly.

Subjective	Objective	Possessive Adjectives	Possessive Pronouns
I	me	my	mine
he	him	his	his
she	her	her	hers
we	us	our	ours
you	you	your	yours
they	them	their	theirs
it	it	its	—

In normal fast speech we often reduce pronouns so that:

him	sounds like	'im
her	sounds like	'er
them	sounds like	'em
he	sounds like	'e
you	sounds like	yə
your	sounds like	yər

PRONUNCIATION ACTIVITY 2

Track 8

A. Listen to the sentences and write the correct pronouns in the blanks. Write the full forms.

1. ___She___ has ___her___ coffee with ___her___ friends

2. _____ tell _____ students _____ stories.

3. _____'re very friendly. I like _____.

4. _____'s very intelligent. Do you like _____?

5. _____ have _____ opinions. Do you agree with _____?

6. _____'s a popular singer. Do you like _____ music?

7. _____'re very quiet. What's _____ name?

8. _____'s a very beautiful picture. Do you like _____?

9. _____'s very talkative. Do know _____? What's _____ name?

10. These books belong to _____. _____'re _____.

B. Now take turns saying the sentences with your partner.

PRONUNCIATION ACTIVITY 3

Track 9

A. Listen to each sentence and then write it.

Questions	Answers
What's her nickname and her surname?	Her nickname is Sandy and her surname is Jones.

Questions	Answers

B. Check your work with your partner and make up answers to the questions. Practise saying the questions and the answers with your partner.

👥 PRONUNCIATION ACTIVITY 4

A. Listen to the sentences and fill in the blanks with the correct words.   🎧 Track 10

1. _____ _____ prettier than _____ sister.
2. _____ _____ richer than _____ parents.
3. _____ _____ smarter than _____ brother.
4. _____ _____ busier than _____ friends.
5. _____ _____ more intelligent than _____ neighbours.
6. _____ _____ hungrier than _____ partner.
7. _____ _____ more interesting than _____ students.
8. _____ _____ more popular than _____ friends.
9. _____ _____ more attractive than _____ mother.

B. Check your work with your partner and practise saying the sentences.

Pronunciation Focus 2: Number of Syllables

👥 PRONUNCIATION ACTIVITY 5

A. Work with a partner and decide how many syllables these words have.   🎧 Track 11

B. Listen to these words and check the number of syllables.

Syllables

happier	_3_	thinner	_____	busiest	_____
interesting	_____	handsome	_____	loudest	_____
shyer	_____	richest	_____	exciting	_____
attractive	_____	talkative	_____		

C. Practise saying the words with your partner. Then make up five sentences using the words and say them to the class.

Pronunciation Focus 3: Contrasting the Sounds /ʌ/ as in *but*, /ʊ/ as in *foot*, and /uw/ as in *true*

PRONUNCIATION ACTIVITY 6

Track 12

A. Listen to each word and repeat it, then put it in the correct box.

two	good	Sunday	funny	ugly	lunch
looks	cook	could	would	hoodie	was
shoe	food	blue	super	you	new
chubby	cousin	cool	who	cute	

/ʌ/ as in *but*	/ʊ/ as in *foot*	/uw/ as in *true*

B. Check your answers with your partner.

C. Use one of the words in the list above in each blank to complete these conversations. You can use some words more than once.

1. How old is your little _____?

   He's _____ and he's very _____.

2. That _____ looks _____ on _____.

   Thanks. _____ is my favourite colour.

3. Who's that in the _____ plaid shirt?

   My boyfriend. _____ you like me to introduce _____?

4. Your running _____ are _____. They _____ very expensive.

   Thank _____. I got them last _____.

5. Who's that _____ _____ guy? He _____ very friendly.

   He's my classmate. I _____ introduce you to him.

6. How was the _____ at _____?

   It was very _____. The _____ is excellent.

D. Practise the conversations with your partner.

PRONUNCIATION ACTIVITY 7

A. Listen to these words. Write *1* if the sound in the word is / ʌ / as in *but,* write *2* if the vowel sound is / ʊ / as in *good,* and write *3* if the sound is / uw / as in *true.*

🎧 **Track 13**

flu	3	soup	_____	suit	_____
luck	1	put	_____	book	_____
cook	2	would	_____	cup	_____
fruit	_____	you	_____	truth	_____
uncle	_____	new	_____	tooth	_____
plump	_____				

B. Work with a partner and make up five sentences using these words. Say your sentences to the class.

COMMUNICATING IN THE REAL WORLD

A. Use your English to talk to people outside your classroom. On your own or with a partner, talk to five people outside your class. Ask them the questions below and record the information. Make a short report to the class about what you learned.

Before you begin, say this:

> May I ask you some questions? This is an assignment for my English class.

1. What's your first name?

2. What's your nickname?

3. What's your favourite girl's name? What's your favourite boy's name?

4. Do you think names are important? Why?

5. What are two adjectives to describe this city?

6. What are two adjectives to describe the people in this city?

7. What do you think is easier: working or studying? Why?

8. What is more important: happiness or money? Why?

B. By yourself or with a partner, go to the website for the city you live in. Find five adjectives to describe your city and life in your city. Report to the class.

SELF-EVALUATION

Think about your work in this chapter. For each row in the chart sections Grammar and Language Functions, Learning Strategies, and Pronunciation, give yourself a score based on the rating scale below and write a comment in the Notes section.

Show the chart to your teacher. Talk about what you need to do to make your English better.

Rating Scale

1	2	3	4	5

Needs improvement. ← → *Great!*

	Score	Notes
Grammar and Language Functions		
using the verb *to be*		
using pronouns		
using adjectives		
using the comparative forms of adjectives		
introducing, greeting, and saying goodbye		
describing people and places		
Pronunciation		
understanding and correctly pronouncing pronouns and contractions		
hearing the difference between and pronouncing the sounds /ʌ/ as in *but*, /ʊ/ as in *good*, and /uw/ as in *true*		
Learning Strategies		
Speaking		
using expressions for introducing, greeting, and saying goodbye, to make my conversations in English easier		
asking for repetition when I don't understand		

Listening

listening for specific information, to help myself understand what I am hearing		
thinking about what I am going to listen to and predicting information that I will hear, to make listening easier.		

Vocabulary and Language Chunks

Look at this list of new vocabulary and language chunks you learned in this chapter. Give yourself a score based on the rating scale and write a comment.

who's who	to make a good impression	common sense
to have on	to have an opinion	the way you look
medium height	the right way	to look on the bright side
wavy hair	on time	to look interesting
baseball cap	to look someone in the eye	
jean jacket	to do your best	

	Score	Notes
understanding new vocabulary and language chunks		
using new words and phrases correctly		

Write six sentences and use new vocabulary you learned in this chapter.

1. _____

2. _____

3. _____

4. _____

5. _____

6. _____

My plan for practising is _____

_____

_____

_____

_____

CHAPTER 2

All in a Day's Work

Routines, Habits, and Occupations

Describing habits and routines

Checking understanding and asking for clarification

Stating reasons

THINKING AND TALKING

Talk about these pictures with a partner. What are these people's jobs?
What do they do every day for a living? Match the pictures to the jobs
and job descriptions below.

1. She's a dog walker. She walks dogs every day for a living.

2. She physiotherapist. She helps people who have injuries and sore miscle.

3. He is a firefigther. He's figthing the fire.

4. She is Kindergarden. She teaches children in a school.

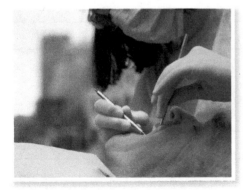

5. She is a dentes. She looks after patients' teeth

6. She is a singer. She sings in a night club or at concerts

7. _She is a doctor. She visites her patiant in the hospital_

8. _He is a plumber. He repairs the pipe_

Job Descriptions	Jobs
1 fixes water pipes and sinks	nurse 2
2 looks after patients in a hospital	physiotherapist 5
3 looks after patients' teeth	singer 7
4 fights fires	teacher 6
5 helps people who have injuries and sore muscles	dentist 3
6 teaches children in a school	dog walker 8
7 sings in a night club or at concerts	plumber 1
8 walks dogs	firefighter 4

When we add the ending –*er* to a verb, it often means a person who does the action.

Examples:

a writer—a person who writes

a traveller—a person who travels

What do these people do for a living?

worker	_is a person who wroxers for a living._
cleaner	_is a person who cleans for a living._
driver	_is a person who drives for a living._
dancer	_is a person who dances for a living._
painter	_is a person who paints for a living._
designer	_is a person who designs for a living._
programmer	_is a person who who programs for a living._

What are three other occupations? What do people with these jobs do for a living?

1. _She is a secretary, she works at the office for a living._
2. _He is a gardener, cultive the land and take care of plants for a living_
3. _She's a designer. She designes clothes for a living._

Grammar Note: Simple Present Tense

We use the simple present tense to talk about repeated actions. We also use it to talk about states or actions that are always true. These are the forms of the simple present tense.

Affirmative	Interrogative	With Question Words
I work.	Do I work?	Why do I work?
You work.	Do you work?	When do you work?
We work.	Do we work?	When do we work?
They work.	Do they work?	Where do they work?
He works.	Does he work?	When does he work?
She works.	Does she work?	Where does she work?
It works.	Does it work?	How does it work?

Negative	Negative Contractions
I do not work.	I don't work.
You do not work.	You don't work.
We do not work.	We don't work.
They do not work.	They don't work.
He does not work.	He doesn't work.
She does not work.	She doesn't work.
It does not work.	It doesn't work.

These are some of the adverbs and adverb phrases used with the simple present tense:

every day	in the mornings	at night
on weekdays	in the afternoon	once a week (month, year)
on Tuesdays	in the evening	twice a year (week, month)

SPEAKING ACTIVITY 1

Work with a partner and read this story. Every time you see a verb in the simple present tense, circle it. Then in the sentences below put the correct form of the verb in the blank. Check your answers with the class.

City Life in Vancouver

Vancouver is Canada's third largest city. It has a population of over 2.3 million. It is one of the world's cleanest cities. Vancouver is on the Pacific Ocean and near the Coast Mountains. Its warm summers and mild winters make it one of the best places to live in Canada or even the world. It is a busy city. On weekdays most people get up between 6:00 AM and 8:00 AM. Many people drive to work every day. Others take public transit, such as buses, ferries, and the SkyTrain. The morning rush hour is from 7:30 to 9:30, when most people hurry to get to work.

Most employees arrive at work at about 9:00 o'clock. They usually work until noon. They get about one hour off for lunch. After lunch, most people work until 5:00 or 6:00 PM. Businesses and offices close at around that time. Then the afternoon rush hour begins as everyone hurries to get home.

In the evenings, Vancouver is fun and exciting. A lot of people go out in the evenings. They go out to dinner at one of Vancouver's excellent restaurants, or they go to movies or plays. Often they go out to a sporting event because Vancouver has hockey, football, baseball, and soccer teams. Some people don't like to go out after a busy day at work. They prefer to stay home and relax. They have supper, watch TV, or get together with friends. Everyone says that life in Vancouver is never boring.

1. Bruce (live) _____lives_____ in Vancouver.

2. He (have) _____has_____ an apartment downtown but he (work) _____works_____ in the suburbs.

3. He (get) _____gets_____ up at 7:30 every morning.

4. He (leave) _____leaves_____ his apartment at 8:30.

5. He usually (take) _____takes_____ the SkyTrain to work.

6. He (get) _____gets_____ to work at 9:00 AM.

7. The people in his company (have) _____have_____ a coffee break at 11:00 AM.

8. They (take) _____take_____ their lunch breaks between 12:00 and 1:00 PM.

9. Bruce (finish) _____finishes_____ work around 5:30.

10. He (arrive) _____arrives_____ home at 6:00 PM.

11. He (check) _____checks_____ his email, (read) _____reads_____ the news and (relax) _____relaxes_____.

12. Bruce and his friends (go) _____*go*_____ out for dinner twice a week.

13. Most of the time he (stay) _____*stays*_____ home and (watch) _____*watches*_____ TV.

14. Sometimes Bruce (buy) _____*buys*_____ tickets for the theatre or a sports event and he (invite) _____*invites*_____ a friend to go with him.

SPEAKING 1

Communication Focus 1: Describing Habits and Routines

We use the simple present tense and adverbs of frequency to talk about habits or routines.

Examples:

Alice is a nurse. She often works at the hospital in the afternoons.

John is a bus driver. He usually drives the Avenue Road bus on weekdays.

Ted is a server. He always works at the restaurant on the weekends.

Anna is a chef. She sometimes plans meals for her restaurant in the mornings.

Grammar Note: Adverbs of Frequency

Adverbs of frequency tell us how often people do things.

Adverb	Meaning
always	100% of the time
usually	80%–90% of the time
often	60%–70% of the time
sometimes	40%–50% of the time
rarely	about 1%–5% of the time
never	0% of the time

Position of adverbs: **after** the verb *to be*   I *was always* on time.
They *are never* late.

before other verbs   Bruce *always gets* to work on time.
They *never arrive* late.

SPEAKING ACTIVITY 2

A. Make a quick chart with the headings shown below. Walk around the room and talk to as many people as possible about their routines. Ask these questions and record the answers. Report to the class about two people.

What do you sometimes do after school?

What do you always do on Saturdays?

What do you never do on weeknights?

What do you often do on weekends?

Name	Sometimes?	Always?	Never?	Often?

B. Write about two classmates.

C. Work with a partner. Use adverbs in these sentences.

1. They take the bus to school. (always)

   They always take the bus to school.

2. Andrea is very happy. (never)

   Andrea is never happy.

4. My friends go out to the movies. (often)

   My friends often go out to the movie.

5. He is tired after work. (usually)

   He is usually tired after work.

6. We take a taxi when we're late. (sometimes)

   We sometime take a taxi when we're late.

7. Students are nervous about tests. (usually)

   Students are usually nervous about tests.

8. Teachers make mistakes. (rarely)

   Teacher rarely make mistakes.

9. Sam sings when he's happy. (always)

   Sam always sings when he's happy.

10. They were relaxed on their holidays. (usually)

   They were usually relaxed on their holidays .

11. They don't speak to their neighbours. (often)

   They don't often speak to their neighbours .

12. She doesn't go out for dinner. (often)

   She doesn't often go out for dinner .

13. Does he apologize? (never)

   Does he never apologize? .

14. Was she busy? (sometimes)

   Was she sometimes busy? .

15. Cats are friendly. (rarely)

   Cats are rarely friendly .

16. Do they drink juice when they're thirsty? (always)   _sediento_

   Do they always drink juices when they're thirsty? .

   ↳ _thirsty (pronoun)_

Grammar Note: Telling Time

These are some ways to tell time.

9:00—nine o'clock

12:00—twelve o'clock

9:50—ten (minutes) to or ten minutes before ten; nine-fifty

6:20—twenty (minutes) after or twenty minutes past six; six-twenty

3:30—three-thirty or half past three

12:30—twelve-thirty or half past ~~four~~ twelve.

10:15—a quarter after or a quarter past ten; ten-fifteen

5:15—a quarter after or a quarter past five; five-fifteen

7:45—a quarter to eight; fifteen minutes to eight; seven-forty-five

2:45—a quarter to three; fifteen minutes to three; two-forty-five

SPEAKING ACTIVITY 3

Answer the questions about your routine and then find out the same information from your partner. Report about your partner.

Questions	Me	My Partner
What time do you get up?	I usually get up at 7:20	
What time do you usually leave for school?	9:00 a.m	
What time do you usually get home after school?		
What time do you usually have dinner?	I usually	
What time do you go to bed?	I us	
What do you do every day?		
How often do you go out to eat?	sometime	
When do you get together with friends?		

SPEAKING ACTIVITY 4

A. Make a quick chart with the headings below. Walk around the room and talk to as many people as possible about their routines. Ask these questions.

How do you usually get home after school?

How long does it usually take you to get home?

What do you often do after school?

Name	How do you usually get home after school?	How long does it usually take you to get home?	What do you often do after school?

B. Write about two classmates.

Communication Focus 2:
Checking Understanding and Asking for Clarification

Sometimes we need to ask questions when we don't understand something. Use these expressions when you don't understand the teacher or your classmates.

I'm sorry, I don't understand. What does _____ He _____ mean?

Could you please say that again?

Could you please explain that?

What does _____ mean?

How do you spell that?

Do you mean _____?

I'm afraid I am not sure what you mean.

I'm sorry. Please explain what you mean.

SPEAKING ACTIVITY 5

Make a quick chart with the headings shown below. Walk around the room and talk to as many people as you can. Find out where people live and what they do. Try to use expressions for checking understanding and asking for clarification when you don't understand people or they don't understand you. Report to the class about three people.

Ask these questions:	Sample answers:
What city do you live in?	I live in Toronto.
What street do you live on?	I live on King Street.
What address do you live at?	I live at 325 King Street.
What do you do on weekdays?	I work in a grocery store every day after school.

Name	City	Street	Address	Activities

LISTENING 1

Before You Listen

PRE-LISTENING ACTIVITY

A. Compare your daily routine with your partner's routine. What things are the same? What is different? Which one of you is busier?

Listening STRATEGY

Working with others on listening tasks lets you share ideas and helps build your confidence. This makes your listening better.

	Me	My Partner
What do you do in the mornings?	I always take a shower	Joaquin usua take a shower
What do you do in the afternoons?	I usually cook the dinner	Aster always eat her lunch
What do you do in the evenings?	I often watch TV programm	He sometimes watches movies

B. With your partner, make a list of three jobs that you think people are very happy in. Explain the reasons for your opinions.

1. _Psycologiste, Barber, hairdresser, Enginier, real state_
2. _Contable, teacher, hospitality (Restaurant, hotel)_
3. _leisure center, comedian, veterinarien animal trainer_

PRE-LISTENING VOCABULARY

A. You will hear a conversation on the audio CD that includes the following words. Work with a partner or by yourself to find the definition of each word.

schedule   ~~crazy~~   ~~marketing~~   soccer   official   photographer

~~volunteer~~   tutoring   council   ~~stuff~~   dangerous   ~~team~~
tutoria   _consejo_   _cosas_   _equipo_

Definitions	Vocabulary
1. a plan or list of activities	**schedule**
2. not safe	dangerous
3. things	stuff
4. not normal, not usual	crazy
5. how to buy and sell things in markets	marketing
6. a game using a ball; European football	soccer
7. a group of people who play or work together for one side	team
8. a person who takes pictures	photographer
9. a person who works without pay	volunteer
10. teaching, giving students extra help	tutoring
11. a group who make decisions	council (cansel)
12. approved by people who have the power	official

B. Choose the correct vocabulary words from the list to fill in the blanks in these sentences. Use each word only once. Not all the words are used in the sentences. Please make changes to the nouns and verbs if necessary.

1. I have a busy ___schedule___ this semester because I am taking an extra course.

2. Julie doesn't get paid for ___tutoring___ students. She's a ___volunteer___.

3. The student ___council___ makes decisions and rules about student life.

4. In ___marketing___ classes people study about how to sell products.

5. She takes pictures for the school newspaper. She's a
   Photographer.

6. A firefighter's job can be _dangerous_.

7. Melanie has a lot of time for reading and other _stuff_.

8. She loves _soccer_. She's _crazy_ about that
   sport.

Listening for the Main Ideas

Listen to the conversation and answer the questions.

 **Track 14**

1. What are the relationships of the speakers? _friends_

2. What are the main topics in the conversation? _school, volunteer, schedule and routines_

3. Where do you think they are?

take shower for breakfast
6:00 eat breakfast
_7:15_
melani soccer team

Listening Comprehension

A. Listen to the conversation as many times as necessary and fill in the
missing information on Julie's schedule.

 **Track 15**

Monday	Tuesday	Wednesday	Thursday	Friday
Morning _every day_ 8:00–10:00 English	**Morning** 8:00–10:00 _English_	**Morning** 8:00–10:00 English	**Morning** 8:00–10:00 _English_	**Morning** 8:00–10:00 _English_
11:00 _Marketing_	11:00 _Marketing_	11:00 _Marketing_	11:00 _Marketing_	11:00 Marketing _every_
Afternoon 1:00–1:30 _lunch_	**Afternoon** 1:00–1:30 lunch	**Afternoon** 1:00–1:30 _lunch_	**Afternoon** 1:00–1:30 _lunch_	**Afternoon** 1:00–1:30 _lunch_
2:00–3:00 _Economic Class_	2:00–3:00 _soccer practices_	2:00–3:00 _e.c_	2:00–3:00 _e.c._	2:00–3:00 _e.c._
3:30–6:30 _soccer practice_	4:00–6:30 _news pept_	3:30–6:30 _volunteer tutoring_	3:30–6:30 _soccer_	3:30–6:00 _student council Juli_
Evening 7:30 _stay home_	**Evening** 7:30 _stay home_	**Evening** 7:30 _stay home_	**Evening** 7:30 _stay home_	**Evening** 7:30 _stay home_
8:00–9:30 _chat with friends_	8:00–9:30 _homework_	8:00–9:30	8:00–9:30	8:00–9:30
10:30	10:30	10:30	10:30	10:30 _bed time_

B. Listen to the conversation again. Write *T* if the statement is true or *F* if it is false.

1. Melanie's schedule is busier than Julie's. ___F___

2. Melanie is reading about which jobs make people the happiest. ___T___

3. Firefighters, teachers, and physiotherapists are some of the people who are happiest in their work. ___T___

4. Writers and artists are not very happy in their jobs. ___F___

5. Julie and Andrew aren't happy about their schedules. ___T___

6. Melanie agrees with them. ___F___

Personalizing

A. With your partner, talk about how you feel about your schedules.

B. Tell your partner about your ideal routine. What time would you like to get up? What would you like to do in the mornings, in the afternoons, and in the evenings? Explain why.

Vocabulary and Language Chunks

Write the number of the expression next to the meaning. After checking your answers, choose five expressions and write your own sentences.

Words and Expressions	Meaning
1. to get up	__1__ to wake up and rise from bed
2. to have lunch/dinner	__5__ time when you have nothing to do
se necesito 3. it takes (time)	__11__ to go somewhere for fun and enjoyment
4. to take transportation	__3__ you need a certain amount of time
5. free time	__10__ to do school work at home
6. to pick up *recoger*	__9__ to want
7. take-out food	__8__ along the route home
8. on the way home	__7__ food you buy and take to eat in another place
9. to feel like	__6__ to get or to buy
10. to do homework	__2__ to eat lunch or dinner
11. to go out	__4__ to use transportation

 SPEAKING ACTIVITY 6

Walk around the room and speak to as many people as you can. Find people who do the following things and write their names down. Report to the class about some of the students you talked to. Use complete sentences.

Make questions like these:

Do you take public transit to school?

Do you eat breakfast every morning?

Find someone who . . .	Name
takes public transit to school.	
doesn't eat breakfast every morning.	
lives far from the school.	
does volunteer work.	
doesn't clean his or her room before he/she leaves for school.	
plays sports after class.	
has a pet.	
doesn't play computer games.	
likes to do homework.	
wants to travel during the next vacation.	
misses his/her family.	
feels homesick.	
doesn't have a TV.	
lives in an apartment.	
goes to bed late.	
goes out on Friday nights.	

SPEAKING ACTIVITY 7

A. Work with a partner. Match the adjectives to the verbs to answer the question:

What do you do when _____?

Make sentences about yourself and your partner.

Example:

When I'm happy, I smile.

happy	cry
sad	smile
thirsty	apologize
lonely	drink something
hungry	go to the doctor
tired	hurry
late	call up a friend
sick	eat something
sorry	rest

B. Use the correct form of the verb *to be* and finish the sentences.

1. When Bruce _____is_____ tired, _____he rests_____.

2. When the students _____ thirsty, _____.

3. When Emma _____ sad, _____.

4. When we _____ hungry, _____.

5. When they _____ sick, _____.

6. When Amanda _____ late, _____.

7. When Marilyn and Jane _____ lonely,
   _____.

8. When Sam _____ sorry, _____.

9. When the clothes _____ dirty, _____.

10. When the children _____ happy, _____.

11. When it _____ cold, _____.

SPEAKING ACTIVITY 8

A. Answer these four questions.

1. What do you do when you are angry? _____

2. What do you do when you are lonely? _____

3. What do you do when you are bored? _____

4. What do you do when you are homesick? _____

B. Make a quick chart with the headings below. Walk around the room and speak to as many people as possible to find out the same information. The teacher will ask you to report about some of the students.

Name	What do you do when you are angry?	What do you do when you are lonely?	What do you do when you are bored?	What do you do when you are homesick?
Carlos	He shouts.	He calls up a friend.	He goes out.	He calls up his mother.

C. Write about two classmates.

When _____ is _____, he/she _____.

LISTENING 2

Before You Listen

PRE-LISTENING ACTIVITIES

A. Work in groups of three. Brainstorm a list of difficult jobs and a list of easy occupations. Explain why you think this. Share your lists with the class.

Difficult Jobs	Reasons	Easy Jobs	Reasons

B. With your group, talk about two specific occupations: video-game designers and astronauts. What do you think is fun and what do you think is difficult about these occupations?

	What's fun?	What's difficult?
Video-game designer		
Astronaut		

PRE-LISTENING VOCABULARY

A. You will hear a program on the audio CD that includes the following words. Work with a partner or by yourself to find the definition of each word.

to create	diploma	typical	graphic art
skills	project	to repair	tasks
computer science	engineer	to replace	strict
experiments	stressful	bones	weightless
deadline	to float	muscles	

flotar

Definitions	Vocabulary
1. to make or produce	**to create**
2. a document from a school, college, or university; a certificate	diploma
3. to fix	to repair
4. to put something in the place of another thing	to replace
5. the hard pieces which form part of a skeleton	bones
6. tissues in the body which produce movement and strength	muscles
7. having no weight	weightless
8. exact, following rules, no changes allowed	strict
9. study of computers and computer technology	computer sciences
10. drawing, painting, print making, any kind of picture	graphic art
11. date or time when everything needs to be finished	deadline
12. scientific tests	experiments
13. average, usual	typical
14. jobs, work	tasks

continued on next page

Definitions	Vocabulary
15. to move slowly or rest on a liquid or in the air	*to float*
16. making a person feel worried and nervous	*stressful → adjective for stress*
17. a person with scientific training who designs and builds machines, products, or systems	*engineer*
18. abilities that come from training and practice	*skills*
19. planned work for a special reason or purpose	*project*

B. Choose the correct vocabulary words from the list to fill in the blanks in these sentences. Use each word only once. Not all the words are used in the sentences. Please make changes to the verbs or nouns if necessary.

1. In the International Space Station, there is no gravity so people and things are __weightless__.

2. A game designer __creates__ video games.

3. Travel in space makes __bones__ and __muscle__ *→ moves (pron.)* weaker. *→ mas débil*

4. Amanda says a game designer doesn't have a __typical__ day because every day is different.

5. Ellen is studying art and design at college because she wants to get a __diploma__ in this.

6. Astronauts often do science __experiments__ in space because they want to test how things work in space.

7. Every day astronauts need to finish all their work or their __tasks__.

8. Astronauts train for many years because they need a lot of knowledge and __skills__.

9. A game designer's work is sometimes very hard and __stressful__.

10. When things are weightless, they __float__ in space.

11. She needs to finish her work by June 30. That's the __deadline__.

12. They can't do whatever they want. They have a very __strict__ schedule to finish the work.

13. The students are working on a __project__ about life in space.

14. When something on the space station stops working, astronauts can __repair__ or __replace__ it.

Listening for the Main Ideas

Track 16   Listen to the program and answer the questions.

que tipo de

1. What kind of show is this? *daily routine the people occupation*
2. What is the show about? *Astronaut experiences*
3. How do the speakers feel about the topic?

Listening Comprehension

Track 17   Listen to the program again as many times as necessary. Write *T* if the statement is true or *F* if it is false.

1. The name of the program is "A Day in The Life." __T__

2. The program is often about video-game designers and astronauts. __F__

3. The video-game developer has a diploma in art. __T__

4. Skills in computer science and graphic art are important for video-game designers. __T__

5. Video-game designers don't have many meetings. __F__

6. Video-game designers work alone for much of the time. __F__

7. A game designer's life is always happy and fun. __F__

8. Astronauts have nothing to do all day. __F__

9. Astronauts follow a strict schedule because they have many tasks to do in space. __T__

10. Astronauts have meetings every day. __T__

11. One problem for astronauts is that everything floats in space. __T__

12. Astronauts only exercise once or twice a week. __F__

13. Astronauts can send tweets and emails from space. __T__

14. Astronauts always do the same jobs on the International Space Station. __F__

15. Astronauts don't have any free time. __F__

Personalizing

1. Work in groups of three and decide as a group which of the occupations in the listening is better and why.

2. Tell each other about two other occupations that each of you likes. Explain why.

3. Tell each other about your career plans. Report to the class about your group.

Vocabulary and Language Chunks

Write the number of the expression next to the meaning. After checking your answers choose five expressions and write your own sentences.

Words and Expressions

1. to be good at
2. to depend on

3. to have a meeting
4. ups and downs *subidas*
5. to meet a deadline
6. time for bed
7. to make a phone call
8. to get ready

9. to wake up
10. to stick to a schedule

subidas y bajadas

Meaning

___1___ to be skilled at

___10___ to follow a plan or list of activities and times

___9___ to become awake

___8___ to prepare

___7___ to telephone

___6___ time at which a person goes to bed

___5___ to finish something on time

___4___ good and bad experiences; pros and cons

___3___ to meet with others

___2___ to be different or to change in different situations

SPEAKING 2

Communication Focus 3: Stating Reasons

We use *because* to explain the reason for an action or state.

Examples:

Dorothy rides her bike to school *because* she doesn't want to drive.

The students eat in the cafeteria *because* they like the food.

Astronauts have a lot of tasks *because* the costs of a space mission are high.

Alison wants to be a video-game designer *because* she's good at computer science.

SPEAKING ACTIVITY 9

A. Work with a partner. Finish the sentences using *because*. Share your sentences with the class.

1. The space station is important because __it helps people learn about space__.

2. Astronauts often do exercises because __they need to use their muscles__.

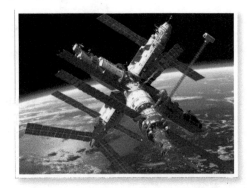

3. Astronauts sometimes do space walks because

_____.

4. Every evening people on the Space Station have meetings because _____.

5. People on the Space Station sometimes look out the window because ___they have a strict shedule_____.

B. Work with a partner. Write five sentences about this picture using *because*. Share your answers with the class.

1. ___People like to play video games because they are fun___

___and entertaining.___

2. _____

3. _____

4. _____

5. _____

SPEAKING ACTIVITY 10

Make a quick chart with the headings below. Walk around the room and talk to as many classmates as possible. Ask these questions.

1. How do you feel about video games? Why do you feel this way?

2. How do you feel about travel in space? Why?

Name	How do you feel about video games?	Reason	How do you feel about travel in space?	Reason

SPEAKING ACTIVITY 11

Work in groups of four. Find the answers to the following riddles. The group that finishes first is the winner.

Example:

What goes up and down the stairs but never moves?   A rug

1. What is the last thing you take off at night before you go to bed?   _____

2. Why do some doctors change jobs?   _____

3. What runs but never walks, has a bed but never sleeps, has a head but never cries, and has a bank but no money?   _____

4. What's the difference between a jeweller and a jailer?   _____

5. What are two days starting with *T*, in addition to Tuesday and Thursday?   _____

PRONUNCIATION

Pronunciation Focus 1: Plurals

PRONUNCIATION ACTIVITY 1

A. The plurals of English nouns have three different pronunciations: / s /, / əz /, and / z /. Listen to each of these nouns and write the sound of the plural ending.   **Track 18**

schedules	__z__	experiences	_____	astronauts	_____
routines	_____	reports	_____	skills	_____
cities	_____	evenings	_____	businesses	_____
nurses	_____	servers	_____	chefs	_____
teams	_____	movies	_____	costs	_____
employees	_____	occupations	_____		

B. Check your answers and then practise saying the plurals with your partner. What is the pronunciation rule?

PRONUNCIATION ACTIVITY 2

A. Work with a partner. What is the pronunciation of the plural in the following words? Put these words into the right place according to the pronunciation of the plural.   **Track 19**

friend	deadline	ticket	sport	experiment	hour
summer	breakfast	lunch	park	student	supper
tree	flower	beach	space	designer	place

Plural Pronounced as /s/	Plural Pronounced as /z/	Plural Pronounced as /əz/
tickets	friends	lunches

B. Listen to the sound of the plural ending of each of these words and check your answers.

C. Make up five sentences with these words and practise saying them with your partner.

PRONUNCIATION ACTIVITY 3

Track 20

A. Listen to the plurals of these words. Write the number of syllables that you hear in each word.

stores	1	offices	_____	spaces	_____
dresses	2	classes	_____	lunches	_____
dogs	_____	nights	_____	cats	_____
days	_____	breaks	_____	buses	_____
juices	_____	pets	_____		

B. Practise saying these words to your partner. Put a check mark next to the plural endings that add an extra syllable.

PRONUNCIATION ACTIVITY 4

Work with a partner. Take turns. One of you will say either sentence (a) or sentence (b). The other partner will listen and say "Singular" or "Plural."
Examples:

Student A: He serves lunch.

Student B: singular

OR

Student A: He serves lunches.

Student B: plural

1. a. Do you have space?
    b. Do you have spaces?

2. a. She has a dog.
    b. She has dogs.

3. a. The neighbours are nice.
    b. The neighbour is nice.

4. a. What classes do you have on Fridays?
    b. What class do you have on Fridays?

5. a. What stores does she shop in?
    b. What store does she shop in?

6. a. They come to school on Wednesday.
    b. They come to school on Wednesdays.

7. a. The nurses like the routines.
    b. The nurse likes the routine.

8. a. He wants to climb the mountains.
    b. He wants to climb the mountain.

9. a. She relaxes in the evenings.
    b. She relaxes in the evening.

10. a. What places do you like to visit?
    b. What place do you like to visit?

11. a. Which vegetables does he want?
    b. Which vegetable does he want?

PRONUNCIATION ACTIVITY 5

A. The third-person singular ending of verbs in the simple present tense also has three pronunciations: / s /, / z /, and / əz /. Listen to the verbs and write the sound of each ending.

Track 21

walks	_s_	rides	_____	misses	_____
studies	_____	washes	_____	drinks	_____
likes	_____	grows	_____	needs	_____
dresses	_____	wants	_____	hurries	_____
works	_____	takes	_____	pushes	_____
tries	_____	eats	_____	cooks	_____

B. Practise saying the verbs with your partner. What is the rule? Then make up five sentences using the verbs.

The pronunciation rule for English plurals is the same for the third-person singular of the simple present tense.

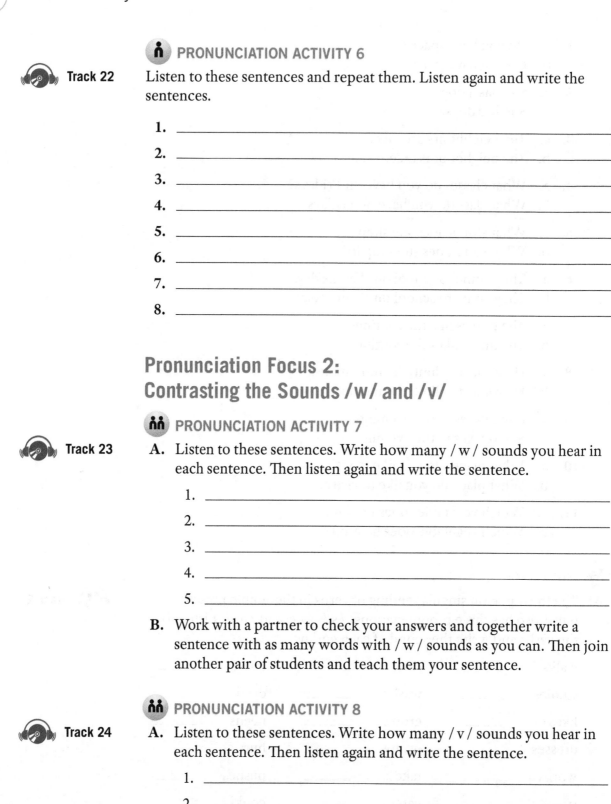

PRONUNCIATION ACTIVITY 6

Track 22

Listen to these sentences and repeat them. Listen again and write the sentences.

1. _____
2. _____
3. _____
4. _____
5. _____
6. _____
7. _____
8. _____

Pronunciation Focus 2: Contrasting the Sounds /w/ and /v/

PRONUNCIATION ACTIVITY 7

Track 23

A. Listen to these sentences. Write how many / w / sounds you hear in each sentence. Then listen again and write the sentence.

1. _____
2. _____
3. _____
4. _____
5. _____

B. Work with a partner to check your answers and together write a sentence with as many words with / w / sounds as you can. Then join another pair of students and teach them your sentence.

PRONUNCIATION ACTIVITY 8

Track 24

A. Listen to these sentences. Write how many / v / sounds you hear in each sentence. Then listen again and write the sentence.

1. _____
2. _____
3. _____
4. _____
5. _____

B. Work with a partner to check your answers and together write a sentence with as many words with / v / sounds as you can. Then join another pair of students and teach them your sentence.

COMMUNICATING IN THE REAL WORLD

A. Use your English to talk to people outside your classroom. On your own or with a partner, talk to five people outside your class. Ask them the questions below and record the information. Make a short report to the class about what you learned.

Before you begin, say this:

> May I ask you some questions? This is an assignment for my English class.

1.   What do you do for a living? Do you like it?

2.   What other job you would like to have?

3.   What's your daily routine? Do you like it?

4.   What schedule or routine would you like to have?

5.   What do you usually feel like doing on the weekend?

6.   How do you feel about video games? What's your favourite game? Why?

7.   What do you usually do when you are angry?

8.   What do you do when you are bored?

B. Make a presentation to the class about your family. Describe the people in your family. Talk about their occupations and their schedules. Answer questions such as the following:

What do they usually do on the weekends?

Do they go on vacations? What do they usually like to do on vacations or holidays?

C. By yourself or with a partner go to websites about occupations. (Your teacher will give you some suggestions.)

Research an occupation that interests you. Make a presentation to the class about this occupation and why it interests you. Answer questions such as the following:

What do people in this occupation do?

What is their daily routine?

What is easy and what is difficult about this occupation?

What are the benefits of doing this job?

SELF-EVALUATION

Think about your work in this chapter. For each row in the chart sections Grammar and Language Functions, Learning Strategies, and Pronunciation, give yourself a score based on the rating scale below and write a comment in the Notes section.

Show the chart to your teacher. Talk about what you need to do to make your English better.

Rating Scale

1	2	3	4	5

Needs improvement. ← ————————————————————— → *Great!*

	Score	Notes
Grammar and Language Functions		
using the simple present tense		
asking questions for clarification when I don't understand		
using adverbs of frequency		
describing habits and routines		
stating reasons		
telling the time		
Pronunciation		
pronouncing the plurals of regular nouns and the third-person singular of the simple present tense		
hearing the difference between /v/ and /w/ and pronouncing these sounds		
Learning Strategies		
Speaking		
practising speaking as much as I can to make myself better at communicating my ideas and at understanding others		
Listening		
working with others on listening tasks to share ideas and help build my confidence to make my listening better		

Vocabulary and Language Chunks

Look at this list of new vocabulary and language chunks you learned in this chapter. Give yourself a score based on the rating scale and write a comment.

to get up	on the way home	ups and downs	to stick to a schedule
to have lunch	to feel like	to meet a deadline	take-out food
it takes (time)	to do homework	to pick up	to wake up
to take transportation	to go out	time for bed	to get ready
free time	to make a phone call	to have a meeting	to depend on

	Score	Notes
understanding new vocabulary and language chunks		
using new words and phrases correctly		

Write six sentences and use new vocabulary you learned in this chapter.

1. _____
2. _____
3. _____
4. _____
5. _____
6. _____

My plan for practising is _____

_____

_____

_____

CHAPTER 3

Easy Come, Easy Go

Shopping, Money, and Numbers

Giving information about
actions in progress

Expressing ability and inability

Expressing ability in the past

Making requests for permission

THINKING AND TALKING

Work with a partner. Label the stores and talk about what they sell. What are people doing there?

Tell your partner about where you shopped in the past week. Discuss your purchases.

LISTENING 1

Before You Listen

PRE-LISTENING VOCABULARY

A. You will hear a conversation on the audio CD that includes the following words. Work with a partner or by yourself to find the definition of each word.

to exchange   refund   mall   outlet

comfortable   department store   discount   advantage

to argue   cash   disadvantage   deal

to purchase   crowds

Definitions	Vocabulary
1. to take one thing in place of another thing	**to exchange**
2. to buy	to purchase
3. getting money back for returning something	refund
4. large groups of people	crowds
5. shopping centre	mall
6. a store in which a company sells its products at cheaper prices	advantage

continued on next page

Definitions	Vocabulary
7. a large store that has separate areas in which they sell different products	*department store*
8. describing something that makes you feel relaxed and at ease	*comfortable*
9. money in bills or coins	*cash*
10. something that is not favourable or good	*disadvantage*
11. a percentage or amount taken off the regular price	*discount*
12. something that is favourable, and is a good thing	*advantage*
13. a bargain *una ganga*	*outlet*
14. to give reasons for or against something; to fight with someone	*to argue*

B. Choose the correct words from the list to fill in the blanks in these sentences. Use each word only once. Not all the words are used in the sentences. Please make changes to the nouns and verbs if necessary.

1. This jacket doesn't fit. I want to ___*exchange*___ it for a bigger size.

2. You can buy many different things in a ___*department store*___ because it has many different sections.

3. This suit is on sale. You can get a 50 percent ___*discount*___ if you buy it.

4. I don't like shopping downtown because there are always huge *enorme* ___*crowds*___ in the stores.

5. Are you paying ___*cash*___ or using a credit card?

6. I can't ___*purchase*___ this coat. It costs too much.

7. If you get this coat at half price, it's a very good ___*deal*___.

8. An ___*outlet*___ is a special kind of store that sells products at much lower prices than in regular stores.

9. We have different ideas about shopping, but I don't want ___*to argue*___ with you. Let's talk about something else.

10. It is easier to shop online. That is an ___*advantage*___.

11. I like going to the ___*mall*___ because there are so many different stores there.

12. Some people think it's more *comfortible* ___*comfortable*___ to shop online.

♟♟♟ PRE-LISTENING ACTIVITY

Work in small groups. Find out the answers to the questions from the others in your group.

Questions	Partner 1	Partner 2
What stores do you usually shop in?	Save on food, Costco, superstore	
What do you buy regularly?	groceries	
What are some things you need to buy?	milk, fruits, vegetables.	
What is your favourite store or way of shopping? Explain why you like it.	my prefer store is costco superstore, because it's cheep and find all	

Listening for the Main Ideas

Listen to the conversation and answer the questions.

 **Track 25**

1. What are Alexa and Sharon talking about? Circle the correct answer.
   a. different stores
   b. different ways of shopping
   c. shopping malls   like to pay cash
   d. different ways of paying
2. What are their opinions about shopping?   always like   It's good shopping online.

Listening Comprehension

Listen to the conversation as many times as necessary and label the statements in this way:

 **Track 26**

O—if the statement is only true for shopping online

S—if the statement is only true for stores

B—if the statement is true about both stores and online shopping

1. You don't need to take a bus or subway. ___O___
2. You can see what clothes look like on you. ___B___
3. You can exchange things and get refunds. ___B___ B
4. You can see and feel the thing you buy. ___S___
5. You don't need to dress up and go out. ___O___
6. It takes less time to buy something. ___O___
7. You don't need to push through crowds. ___O___
8. You can shop around and compare prices and styles. ___B___ B
9. You can pay in cash. ___S___
10. You can get a discount. ___O___ B
11. You can ask for a discount. ___S___
12. You can ask the sales clerk for an opinion. ___S___

Personalizing

Work with a small group. Discuss the following. Present your answers to the class.

1. Which is better: shopping in malls or shopping online? Explain why.

2. What are some stores where you can get discounts in this city?

Vocabulary and Language Chunks

Write the number of the expression next to the meaning. After checking your answers choose five expressions and write your own sentences.

Words and Expressions	Meanings
1. to look for	__2__ to examine
2. to look at	__1__ to search for, to try to find
3. to try on	__6__ to buy something at a lower, cheaper price
4. to put on	__5__ to compare different styles and prices in many stores
5. to shop around	__3__ to put clothes on to see if they fit
6. to get a good deal	__7__ to stay in one place until someone or something arrives
7. to wait for	__8__ an expression we use to add another piece of information
8. by the way	__4__ to dress in something
9. to be up to	__9__ to be doing an activity

👥 SPEAKING ACTIVITY 1

Work with a partner and find out the answers to the following questions about shopping in this city and shopping in other countries. Report to the class about your partner.

1. Do most people in your hometown shop in malls, in small stores, or online? Explain why.

2. Are prices for food and groceries cheaper or more expensive in your hometown than prices here?

3. Are prices for clothes and jewellery lower in your hometown than prices here?

4. Compare the stores in your hometown with the stores here. (bigger, smaller, or ?)

5. Compare the service in stores in your hometown to service in stores here.

6. Which do you like better, shopping in Canada or shopping in your home country? Explain why.

👥 SPEAKING ACTIVITY 2

Look at the following proverbs or sayings. Talk about the meanings of the proverbs with your partner. Do you agree with them?

What proverbs about money are there in your language? Explain them.

Proverbs	Meaning	Agree?	Other Proverbs
A penny saved is a penny earned.			
Money isn't everything.			
Money talks.			
You can't take it with you.			
The best things in life are free.			

👥 SPEAKING ACTIVITY 3

Look at the pie chart of a student's budget. Compare it to your budget. What are some differences? What do you spend more on? What do you spend less on? Then make a pie chart of your spending. With your partner talk about some differences between your budget and the average student's budget.

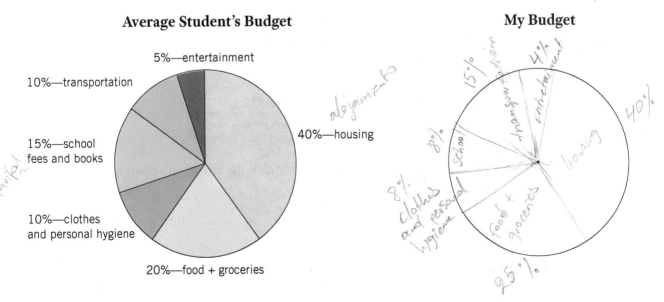

Average Student's Budget

5%—entertainment
10%—transportation
15%—school fees and books
10%—clothes and personal hygiene
20%—food + groceries
40%—housing

My Budget

SPEAKING 1

Communication Focus 1:
Giving Information about Actions in Progress

We use the present progressive tense to talk about actions in progress or continuing actions.

Actions in Progress

I'm checking my email now.

We're listening to the teacher at this moment.

She isn't talking on her cellphone right now.

Continuing Actions

John's looking for a job at this time.

We're saving money to buy a house.

They aren't renting an apartment. They are staying with her parents.

Grammar Note: The Present Progressive Tense

These are the forms of the present progressive (or present continuous) tense.

Affirmative	Contractions	Interrogative
I am working.	I'm working.	Am I working?
You are working.	You're working.	Are you working?
We are working.	We're working.	Are we working?
They are working.	They're working.	Are they working?
He is working.	He's working.	Is he working?
She is working.	She's working.	Is she working?
It is working.	It's working.	Is it working?

Negatives	Contractions
I am not working.	I'm not working.
You are not working.	You aren't working.
We are not working.	We aren't working.
They are not working.	They aren't working.
He is not working.	He isn't working.
She is not working.	She isn't working.
It is not working.	It isn't working.

These time expressions usually require the use of the present progressive tense:

now	at the present time	at this time	at this moment
this week	this year	today	

ii SPEAKING ACTIVITY 4

Make up sentences to answer the questions. Work with a partner and share your answers. Report to the class about your partner.

1. What are three things you are doing at this moment?

   a. _____

   b. _____

   c. _____

2. What are three people in your class doing right now?

   a. _____

   b. _____

   c. _____

3. Write about two people not in your class. What are they doing now?

   a. _____

   b. _____

ii SPEAKING ACTIVITY 5

What are actions that you sometimes do but you are not doing now? Write five sentences about yourself. Share your work with your partner. What is the same and what is different about you and your partner?
Example:

> I sometimes listen to music, but I'm not listening to music at this moment.

1. _____

2. _____

3. _____

4. _____

5. _____

iii SPEAKING ACTIVITY 6

Make a quick chart with the headings shown below. Walk around the room and talk to as many people as you can. Ask these questions. Report the most interesting answers to the class.

Names	What is your best friend's name?	Where is your best friend now?	What is your best friend doing at this time?

Write about two classmates.

SPEAKING ACTIVITY 7

inventa una historia

With your partner, make up a story about one of these pictures. Where are the people? What are some of them doing? What are others doing? Why are they doing this? Tell your story to another pair of students and listen to their story.

1.   2.   3.   4.

SPEAKING ACTIVITY 8

Make questions and find the people who fit these descriptions. Write their names. Report to the class about one person.

Example:

Are you looking for a new place to live at this time?

Find someone who . . .	Name
is looking for a new place to live at this time.	Are you looking
is saving money for a special reason.	Are you saving money?
is working part time.	Are you working part-time?
is looking for a part-time job.	Are you looking for a part-time job?
is taking driving lessons.	Are you taking driving lesson?
is wearing a sweater.	Are you wearing a sweater?
is wearing black socks.	Are you wearing a black...?
is taking another course.	Are you taking another course?
is using a dictionary.	Are you using a dictionary
is wearing a necklace.	Are you wearing a neckles
is thinking about the weekend.	Are you thinking about the weekend?
is wearing running shoes.	Are you wearing running shoes?
is planning to go shopping soon.	Are you planning to go shopping soon?

SPEAKING ACTIVITY 9

A. Work with a partner. Make sentences using the present progressive tense.

B. Read your sentences to another pair to see if they are correct.

1. Many people / do / their Christmas shopping / now.

   Many people are doing their Christmas shopping now.

2. They / look for / bargains / in the department stores.

   They are looking for bargins in the department stores.

3. They / get / discounts on toys and clothes and other gifts.

   They are getting discounts on toys and clothes and other gifts.

4. My sister / shop / for socks for everyone in our family.

   My sister is shopping for socks for everyone in our family.

5. I / wait / for the last-minute sales just before Christmas.

   I am waiting for the last-minutes sales just before christmas.

6. Who / you / buy / presents for this year?

   who are you buying presents for this year?

7. My best friend / not buy / any presents this year because she / save / money for a trip during the Christmas vacation.

   My best friends is not buying any presents this year because she is saving money for a trip during the Christmas vacation.

Communication Focus 2: Expressing Ability and Inability

We use the modal *can* to express ability.

Examples:

Affirmative	Interrogative	Negative
I <u>can speak</u> English.	<u>Can</u> you <u>speak</u> French?	She <u>can't speak</u> Japanese.
We <u>can walk</u> to school.	They <u>can't use</u> cellphones.	<u>Can</u> he <u>spell</u> the word?

PRONUNCIATION ACTIVITY 1

Can't is stressed in English. We say it louder and longer than *can*. *Can* is not stressed in English. Don't stress *can* because people will think you are saying *can't*.

 **Track 27**

Listen to the following sentences. Which word do you hear? Write *can* or *can't* and the verb in each blank.

1. _Can ask_   5. _Can purchase_   9. _can get_
2. _can't exchange_   6. _Can't get_   10. _Can you show_
3. _Can park_   7. _Can pay / can use_ 11. _can / cash a cheq_
4. _Money can't buy_ 8. _can't argue_   12. _can't afford_

SPEAKING ACTIVITY 10

Do this activity by yourself first. Make statements about your abilities and inabilities using the following verbs. Then work with a partner to find out about him or her, and report some interesting information to the class.
Examples:

speak   I can speak English, but I can't speak Spanish.

ride   I can ride a bicycle, but I can't ride a horse.

1. cook   _I can cook colombian food_, but _I can't cook gourtme_.
2. sing   _I can sing at home_, but _I can't sing in public_.
3. write   _I can write a letters_, but _I can't write poems_.
4. dance   _I can dance salsa_, but _can't dance tango_.
5. use   _I can use pantalons_, but _can't use short_.
6. understand _I can understand French_, but _Can't understand arabic_.
7. make   _I can make pasta_, but _Can't make suchi_.
8. do   _I can do laundry_, but _can't do the dishes_.
9. drink   _I can drink coffee_, but _I can't drink black tea_.
10. carry   _I can carry small stuff_, but _I can't carry heavy stuff_.
11. other: _I can eat pork_, but _I can't eat beef_.
12. other: _____, but _____.

SPEAKING ACTIVITY 11

Work in groups of four. Find out the answers to these questions from your partners. Report to the class about things you have in common.

What two things can you do very well?

What two things can't you do very well?

What two things can you afford to buy?

What two things can't you afford to buy?

	Can Do Very Well	Can't Do Very Well	Can Afford	Can't Afford
Me				
Partner 1				
Partner 2				
Partner 3				

SPEAKING ACTIVITY 12

Make a quick chart with the headings shown below. Walk around the room and talk to as many students as you can. Ask the following questions.

What languages can you speak?

What sport or game can you play?

What special ability do you have?

Name	Languages	Sport or Game	Special Ability

SPEAKING ACTIVITY 13

Make questions and find the people who fit these descriptions. When you find a person who matches a description, ask him or her to write his or her name in the box. Report to the class about two people.

Examples:

Can you ride a bicycle?   How many languages can you speak?

can ride a bicycle	can't swim	can play an instrument	can speak three or more languages
can play tennis	can't afford to buy a new car	can say "I love you" in three languages	can jog for one kilometre
can't walk to school	can whistle	can't draw	can bake a cake
can cook Chinese food	can sew	can take good pictures	can walk to school

SPEAKING ACTIVITY 14

Work in groups of four. Find the answers to these riddles. The group who finishes first is the winner.

Example:

What has four legs but can't walk?   a table

1. What can go around the world but stays in a corner?
2. What has hands but can't clap?
3. What has 88 keys but can't open any door?
4. What instrument can you hear but can never see?
5. What has holes but can hold a lot of water?

Communication Focus 3: Expressing Ability in the Past

We use the modal *could* to talk about ability in the past.

Examples:

Customers <u>can use</u> credit cards.

Customers <u>could use</u> credit cards last year.

You <u>can't get</u> a discount in a department store.

You <u>couldn't get</u> a discount in a department store before.

Anna <u>can skate</u> very well.

Anna <u>could skate</u> when she was a child.

Affirmative	**Interrogative**	**Negative**
She <u>could dance</u> very well.	<u>Could</u> he <u>draw</u>?	We <u>couldn't see</u> the picture.

SPEAKING ACTIVITY 15

Work in groups of four. Ask these questions.

What could you buy in your hometown that you can't buy now?

What couldn't you buy in your hometown that you can buy now?

What could you do in your hometown that you can't do now?

What couldn't you do in your hometown that you can do now?

	Could Buy?	Couldn't Buy?	Could Do?	Couldn't Do?
Me				
Partner 1				
Partner 2				
Partner 3				

LISTENING 2

Before You Listen

Listening STRATEGY 🦻

Think about what you already know about a topic to help your listening comprehension of lectures or other listening selections.

👥 **PRE-LISTENING ACTIVITY 1**

Work with a partner and discuss these questions. Report the most interesting answers to the class.

Questions	Me	My Partner
What is the name of the money people use in your home country?		
How is it different from the money we use here?		
How do most people pay for things in your home country—cash, credit card, or _____? Explain why.		
What is the value of your home country's money compared to North American money?		
What is more expensive in your hometown?		
What is cheaper in your hometown?		
How do you think people will pay for things in the future?		

👥 **PRE-LISTENING ACTIVITY 2**

Work with a partner. Match the pictures with the words in the list. Which of these do people use as money? Where do people use this kind of money? Report your ideas to the class.

1. shells
2. paper banknotes (bills)
3. gold coins
4. cows

_____   _____   _____   _____

PRE-LISTENING VOCABULARY

You will hear a lecture on the audio CD that includes the following words. Work with a partner or by yourself to find the definition of each word.

valioso   *Intercambiar*   *divisa*   *trueque*   *ganado*
valuable   to trade   currency   to barter   cattle   salary

inteligente
clever   metal   leather   gold   silver
                            oro

cadena
string   to farm   vase
        cosechar   *florero*

Definitions	Vocabulary
1. costs a lot of money	valuable
2. to exchange one thing for another	to trade
3. money that people earn by working	salary
4. system of money	currency
5. a long thin piece of cord or thread which we use to tie things together	string
6. cows that farmers keep and raise	cattle
7. to exchange things or services for others of the same value	to barter
8. to make a living by growing food or raising animals	to farm
9. a hard element from nature	metal
10. very valuable yellow metal	gold
11. strong material made from animal skin	leather
12. smart, intelligent	clever
13. a container made of glass or porcelain, often used to put flowers in	vase
14. valuable, bright, light grey metal	silver

Choose the correct words from the list to fill in the blanks in these sentences. Use each word only once. Not all the words are used in the sentences. Please make changes to the nouns and verbs if necessary.

1. Can I see the ____leather____ sandals on the top shelf?

2. A sales clerk doesn't make a lot of money. He gets a low __salary__.

3. Some people exchange goods and services with each other. They don't use money. They prefer __to barter__.

4. I like your new coat better than mine. Do you want __to trade__?

5. The name of the __currency__ that people use in France and Germany is the euro.

6. I want to exchange this plastic cover for a __metal__ one. It's stronger.

7. They grow fruits and vegetables. They __farm__ a large piece of land.

8. Long ago people used _____*gold*_____ or _____*Silver*_____ coins as money.

9. He is very smart and his sister is also a _____*Clever*_____ person.

10. That ring is made of gold. I think it's very _____*Valuable*_____.

Listening for the Main Ideas

Listen to the lecture and answer the questions.   🎧 **Track 28**

1. This lecture is about:
   a. ways of exchanging money.
   b. the changes in money over thousands of years.
   c. the kind of money people use in different countries.

2. The professor sometimes asks questions because:
   a. he wants the students to think about the ideas.
   b. he wants the students to be part of the lecture.
   c. he doesn't want the students to be bored.
   d. All of the above.

3. What country was important in the development of money in ancient times? *CHina*

Listening Comprehension

A. Listen to the lecture again as many times as necessary and number the items in the order that the professor talks about them.   🎧 **Track 29**

leather money	3
silver coins	6
credit cards	7
coins with holes in them	4
shells	2
bills	5
bartering	1

B. Write *T* if the statement is true or *F* if it is false.

The lecture tells us:

1. Currency means the same thing as money. __T__

2. To barter is to trade things. __T__

3. No one barters today. __T__

4. The word *salary* comes from the word *salt* because people traded salt for things. __T__

5. Shells were the first kind of money in many countries. __T__

6. People started to make coins because they could not find enough shells. _T_

7. People first started to use coins over 3,000 years ago. _T_

8. The first Chinese coins had holes in the middle. _T_

9. The first coins had pictures of kings on them. _F_

10. The first kind of banknote came from India. _F_

11. The first people to use paper money were Europeans. _F_

12. Canadians use one-cent coins and two-dollar bills. _F_

13. Credit cards started in America and Europe. _T_

Personalizing

Discuss these questions in groups. Report to the class.

1. When do you use each of these: credit cards, debit cards, cash? Which do you think is the best? Explain why.

2. What good or bad experiences have you had using credit cards, debit cards, or cash?

3. How important is money to you? Explain.

4. A famous person said: "I've been rich and I've been poor and, believe me, rich is better." Do you agree? Why or why not?

Vocabulary and Language Chunks

Write the number of the expression next to the meaning. After checking your answers choose five expressions and write your own sentences.

Words and Expressions

1. that's right
2. what's wrong with *con*
3. to come from *venir*
4. to jump ahead *saltar adelante*
5. the first step
6. to carry around
7. right on *tocar el asunto exacto*
8. to give someone an idea *darle alguien*
9. over time *con el tiempo*
10. after a while *despues de un rato*

Meanings

_3_ to start in, to originate in

_7_ exactly correct

_6_ to take from place to place *llevar de un lugar a otro*

_2_ what is the problem with

_10_ after some time *despues de un tiempo*

_4_ to go ahead, to go forward *ir hacia adelante*

_9_ after a very long period of time, through the years

_5_ the beginning point, the first thing to do

_1_ that is correct

_8_ to make someone think about something

SPEAKING 2

Communication Focus 4:
Making Requests for Permission

We use these grammar structures to make requests for permission.

Structure	Example	Possible Response
Could I + base form of the verb	Could I try on these pants?	Of course. The fitting room is over there.
May I + base form of the verb	May I use your pen?	Sure, no problem.
Can I + base form of the verb	Can I pay by cheque?	No, I'm sorry. We don't accept personal cheques.

SPEAKING ACTIVITY 16

Work with a partner. Think about some of the things you do in a bank. Look at the list below. Write out the request for each one. Then practise making the request and responding to it.

1. open an account _____ Could I open a savings account? _____
2. see the manager _____ *May I see the manager?* _____
3. make an appointment with the loan officer *Could I make an appointment... ?*
4. certify a cheque _____ *may I certify cheque ?* _____
5. fill out a change-of-address form _____ *Could I fill out a change-of-address form*
   completor un
6. exchange some American currency *may/could I exchange some America currency ?*
7. apply for a credit card *could/may apply for a credit card?*
8. get a replacement card *could/may I get a replacement card ?*
9. get a debit card *could /may I get a debit card ?*
10. sign up for online banking _____ *could I sing up for online banking ?*

SPEAKING ACTIVITY 17

1. Work with a partner to practise the conversations below.

   Person A: Hi, Ann. May I use your cellphone to call my mom? She's coming to pick me up and I'm late.

   Person B: Sure no problem. Here you go.

   Person A: Hi, Fred. Could I borrow $20 from you until next week? I'm broke!

   Person B: I'm sorry, George. I can't lend you any money. I'm short of cash myself.

2. Make new conversations requesting permission about some of the following:

dictionary	eraser	calculator
laptop	pencil sharpener	scissors
$100	textbook	notes from our last class

Speaking STRATEGY

If someone doesn't understand, use other ways to make your meaning clear. You can write numbers or words, or draw pictures.

SPEAKING ACTIVITY 18

Work in small groups. Brainstorm some requests for permission that students sometimes make. The group with the longest list of student requests is the winner.

Example:

May I write the test in pencil?

Grammar Note: Cardinal Numbers

These are the cardinal numbers in English:

Numbers	Words	Numbers	Words
1	one	19	nineteen
2	two	20	twenty
3	three	30	thirty
4	four	31	thirty-one
5	five	41	forty-one
6	six	52	fifty-two
7	seven	63	sixty-three
8	eight	74	seventy-four
9	nine	85	eighty-five
10	ten	96	ninety-six
11	eleven	100	one hundred
12	twelve	1,000	one thousand
13	thirteen	1,200	one thousand, two hundred OR twelve hundred
14	fourteen	10,000	ten thousand
15	fifteen	11,350	eleven thousand three hundred and fifty
16	sixteen	99,999	ninety-nine thousand, nine hundred, and ninety-nine
17	seventeen	100,000	one hundred thousand
18	eighteen	1,000,000	one million

ÀÀ SPEAKING ACTIVITY 19

Work with a partner. Ask each other these questions and write the answers in the chart.

Questions	Me	My Partner
How old are you?		
What year were you born?		
What is your street address?		
How many students are there in this class?		
How many students are there in this school?		
What is the population of this city?		
What is the population of your hometown?		
What is the population of this country?		
What is the population of the country you came from?		
What is the population of the world?		
Do you have a lucky number? What is it? Explain why it's lucky.		

Grammar Note: Ordinal Numbers

These are the ordinal numbers in English:

Cardinal Numbers	Ordinal Numbers	Cardinal Numbers	Ordinal Numbers
1	first	21	twenty-first
2	second	30	thirtieth
3	third	32	thirty-second
4	fourth	40	fortieth
5	fifth	44	forty-fourth
6	sixth	55	fifty-fifth
7	seventh	66	sixty-sixth
8	eighth	77	seventy-seventh
9	ninth	100	one hundredth
10	tenth	101	one hundred and first
11	eleventh	1,000	one thousandth
12	twelfth	1,501	fifteen hundred and first
13	thirteenth	1,000,000	one millionth
20	twentieth		

SPEAKING ACTIVITY 20

Play this game with a group. When someone makes a mistake, that person is out. The winner is the person who has not made any mistakes.

Everyone in your group counts off using cardinal numbers, except for every fifth person who must use the ordinal number. For example, one, two, three, four, **fifth**, six, seven, eight, nine, **tenth**. Continue until someone makes a mistake. He/she is out. Start again from one. To make the game a little more difficult, change the number to seven. For example, one, two, three, four, five. six, **seventh**, eight, nine, ten, eleven, twelve, thirteen, **fourteenth**.

PRONUNCIATION

Pronunciation Focus 1: The Sounds /ɪ/ and /iy/

PRONUNCIATION ACTIVITY 2

heat　hit

Track 30　Listen and circle the number that you hear.
Example:

15　(50)　51

a.	30	(13)	33	f.	(90)	19	919
b.	70	77	(17)	g.	(150)	155	115
c.	18	(80)	81	h.	39	(93)	33
d.	(60)	66	16	i.	770	(717)	777
e.	(114)	140	144	j.	(330)	13	30

PRONUNCIATION ACTIVITY 3

Track 31　**A.** Listen to the numbers and write them.
Example:

$ 717.27

1. _____ _____
2. _____ _____
3. _____ _____
4. _____ _____
5. _____ _____
6. _____ _____
7. _____ _____
8. _____ _____
9. _____ _____
10. _____ _____

B. Check your answers with your partner and the class.

C. Write the amounts out in words.
Example:

$ 717.27   seven hundred and seventeen dollars and
              twenty-seven cents

Practise saying them to your partner.

👥 **PRONUNCIATION ACTIVITY 4**

A. Listen and underline the word that you hear in each pair.   🎧 Track 32
Example:

seat   <u>sit</u>

1. (heat)	hit		8. (leap)	lip
2. sheep	ship		9. (mitt)	meat
3. (fit)	feet		10. (teen)	tin
4. sleep	(slip)		11. beat	(bit)
5. weep	(whip)		12. cheap	(chip)
6. (Pete)	pit		13. (eat)	it
7. (deep)	dip			

B. Check your answers. Practise saying the words with your partner
and then make up five sentences using some of these words.

👥 **PRONUNCIATION ACTIVITY 5**

A. Listen to the sentences and write the missing words in the blanks.   🎧 Track 33
Example:

Please don't <u>sit</u> in her <u>seat</u>.

1. Do those boots __*fit*__ her __*feet*__ ?

2. __*Pete*__ never eats the __*pit*__ .

3. How many __*ship*__ are on the __*sheap*__ ?

4. He sometimes __*slips*__ off the bed in his __*sleep*__ .

5. The __*heat*__ just __*hits*__ you when you open the door.

6. They __*weep*__ when they see the __*whip*__ .

7. Don't __*dip*__ your spoon so __*deep*__ into the jam.

8. Don't bite your __*lip*__ when you __*leap*__ .

9. Don't put your __*mitt*__ on the __*meat*__ .

10. A __*teen*__ can eat two __*teen*__ of sardines.

11. Please take a __*seat*__ and __*sit*__ until she calls you.

12. Can you __beat__ the eggs a little __bit__ ?

13. I don't like those __cheap__ __chips__ .

14. He doesn't __eat__ __it__ all the time.

B. Check your answers and practise saying the sentences with your partner.

Pronunciation Focus 2: The Sounds /l/ and /r/

🛉🛉 PRONUNCIATION ACTIVITY 6

Track 34

A. Listen and underline the word that you hear in each pair.

clouds	crowds		grass	glass
late	rate		collect	correct
free	flee		load	road
blush	brush		right	light
wrist	list		lush	rush
rain	lane		pirate	pilot
brew	blue		fly	fry
clown	crown		blue	brew
locker	rocker			

B. Check your work and practise saying all the words with your partner.

C. Use some of the words to complete the conversations below.

1. Look at the time! It's five-thirty. I'm really __later__.

   Are you __free__ tomorrow afternoon? I can help you __correct__ your grammar mistakes then.

2. Why are you in such a __rush__ ?

   I want to get home and cut the __grass__ while it's still __rain__ out.

3. Could I borrow your __blue__ sweater?

   Okay. It's in my __locker__ . I can get it for you.

4. Why are you __blushing__ ?

   I'm nervous. That __clown__ is looking __right__ at me.

5. What's wrong with your __wrist__ ?

   I hurt myself when I tried to __load__ the boxes on the truck.

6. Excuse me. Is this the __right__ __road__ to the shopping mall?

   It sure is. See, there are huge __crowds__ up ahead!

7. Do you see all the ___Clouds___? I think it's going to ___rain___.

   Don't worry about the weather. Let's ___brew___ some tea and relax.

8. What does your brother do for a living?

   He's a ___pilot___.

   You mean he ___flies___ planes?

   Yes. He's a clever guy.

D. Check your answers with the class. Practise the conversations.

E. Make up five sentences using as many of the words as you can. Practise saying the sentences. Then join another pair of students and teach them your sentences.

COMMUNICATING IN THE REAL WORLD

A. Use your English to talk to people outside your classroom. On your own or with a partner, talk to five people outside your class. Ask them the questions below and record the information. Make a short report to the class about what you learned.

Before you begin, say this:

> May I ask you some questions? This is an assignment for my English class.

1. What's the best area to shop in, in this city?

2. What do you think is expensive in this city?

3. Which do you think is better: shopping in malls or shopping online? Please explain why.

4. Do you think it's a good idea to shop around when you need to buy clothes?

5. Do you know any stores that give discounts in this city?

6. Are women better shoppers than men? What do you think?

7. What things are more important than money?

8. A famous person said: "I've been rich and I've been poor and, believe me, rich is better." Do you agree? Why or why not?

B. By yourself or with a partner, go to the website of a big store in your city. What information did you learn about the store? Read some of the ads and write down eight new words and find their definitions. Report to the class.

C. Project: Work with a partner. It's your job to find and buy furniture for your bedroom. You need to buy a bed and night table, a desk and chair, a dresser, an armchair, and a TV. You can only spend a maximum of 1,000 dollars. Try to spend as little as possible.

You can

- search buy-and-sell websites (Your teacher will give you some suggestions.)
- go to garage sales
- visit department stores (online or in person) to find the furniture.

Make a poster and report to the class about your research and what you can buy.

SELF-EVALUATION

Think about your work in this chapter. For each row in the chart sections Grammar and Language Functions, Learning Strategies, and Pronunciation, give yourself a score based on the rating scale below and write a comment in the Notes section.

Show the chart to your teacher. Talk about what you need to do to make your English better.

Rating Scale

1	2	3	4	5

Needs improvement. ← ———————————————————————→ *Great!*

	Score	Notes
Grammar and Language Functions		
talking about stores and shopping		
using the present progressive tense		
describing actions in progress and continuing actions		
using *can/can't* to describe abilities in the present and *could/couldn't* to describe abilities in the past		
asking for permission		
using cardinal and ordinal numbers		
Pronunciation		
hearing the difference between and pronouncing the sounds /ɪ/ and /iy/		
hearing the difference between and pronouncing the sounds /l/ and /r/		

Learning Strategies

Speaking

exchanging ideas with others in English to motivate myself to speak English more		
writing out words or numbers or drawing pictures if someone doesn't understand me		

Listening

thinking about what I already know about a topic to help my comprehension of lectures or other listening selections		

Vocabulary and Language Chunks

Look at this list of new vocabulary and language chunks you learned in this chapter. Give yourself a score based on the rating scale and write a comment.

look for	shop around	by the way
to be up to	look at	get a good deal
that's right	jump ahead	try on
what's wrong with	the first step	over time
put on	wait for	come from
carry around	right on	give someone an idea
after a while		

	Score	Notes
understanding new vocabulary and language chunks		
using new words and phrases correctly		

Write six sentences and use new vocabulary you learned in this chapter.

1. _____
2. _____
3. _____
4. _____
5. _____
6. _____

My plan for practising is _____

_____

_____

_____

_____

Let Me Entertain You

Leisure Activities, Interests, and Hobbies

CHAPTER 4

- Expressing likes and dislikes
- Starting and closing conversations
- Giving instructions
- Making general requests

THINKING AND TALKING

Look at these pictures with a partner. What are people doing for entertainment?

Choose from the following list.

They are watching a ballet.

He is playing an instrument.

Some people are playing video games.

She is listening to music.

They are dancing.

She is singing in a karaoke bar.

They are listening to music at a concert.

Make a list of activities you like to do for entertainment and relaxation. Share your list with the class.

SPEAKING 1

Communication Focus 1: Expressing Likes and Dislikes

We use the following structures to express likes.

Structure/Expression	Examples	
like	I like concerts.	I like going to concerts.
love	Sharon loves music.	Sharon loves listening to music.
enjoy	Howard enjoys video games.	Howard enjoys playing video games.
be crazy about *estar loco por*	They are crazy about karaoke.	They are crazy about going to karaoke.
feel like *tener ganas de*	Do you feel like a movie?	Do you feel like going to a movie?

We use these expressions to express dislikes.

Structure/Expression	Examples	
don't like	John doesn't like horse races.	John doesn't like watching horse races.
hate	Mike hates dances.	Mike hates going to dances.
can't stand	Emily can't stand ballet.	Emily can't stand going to ballets.
don't feel like	We don't feel like pizza.	We don't feel like having pizza.
dislike	Anne dislikes soccer.	Anne dislikes playing soccer.

Grammar Note: Gerunds

Some verbs in English can only be followed by a gerund or a noun. The gerund is the base form of the verb + -ing, for example, *going, singing,* or *dancing*.

Some verbs that require gerunds are *enjoy, avoid, miss, dislike, practise, finish, feel like*.

Examples:

She finished her homework. She finished doing her homework.

Ellen enjoys action movies. She enjoys watching action movies.

I miss my friends in Paris. I miss seeing my friends in Paris.

We avoid mistakes. We avoid making mistakes.

SPEAKING ACTIVITY 1

Practise this conversation with a partner, then together make up three conversations about the places and activities below.

Person A: How about going to the museum after school today? They have an exhibit of old coins.

Person B: I don't feel like going to the museum. It's a beautiful day and I don't want to be inside.

Person A: Okay. Let's go jogging in the park.

Person B: I can't stand jogging. It's boring.

Person A: Well, what do you enjoy doing?

Person B: I feel like going to the amusement park. I'm crazy about going on the rides.

Person A: Me too. I love excitement. Okay, let's go.

theatre	baseball game	museum	beach
movie theatre	soccer game	art gallery	gym
opera	go biking	zoo	hockey game
concert	go swimming	aquarium	ice skating rink
ballet	go skating	park	volleyball game

SPEAKING ACTIVITY 2

Work in groups of four. Ask each other the questions below. What are some similarities and differences among you? Report to the class about your group.

1. What are you crazy about?
2. What can't you stand?
3. What do you usually feel like doing on weekends?
4. What do you want to practise doing?
5. What do you miss doing?

Speaking STRATEGY

If you check the language you are producing to see if others can understand you, your speaking will get better.

Grammar Note: Infinitives

Some verbs in English can only be followed by infinitives. The infinitive is the base form of the verb with *to*, for example, *to work, to study, to dance.*

A few of the verbs that require infinitives are *want, need, plan, hope, decide, learn, would like.*

Examples:

Affirmative	Question Forms
The students want to have a picnic.	Do the students want to have a picnic?
Everyone needs to study for the English test.	Does everyone need to study for the English test?
Jeremy plans to go to the gym after school.	Does Jeremy plan to go to the gym after school?
Mary is learning to ski this winter.	Is Mary learning to ski this winter?
I would like to go to a basketball game.	Would you like to go to a basketballgame?
They hope to pass the test.	Do they hope to pass the test?

SPEAKING ACTIVITY 3

Walk around the room and ask questions to find people who fit the following descriptions.

Find someone who. . .	Name
likes to play video games.	
hopes to get married someday.	
likes to sing in the shower.	
wants to learn to dance.	

continued on next page

Find someone who. . .	Name
wants to learn to play an instrument.	
wants to meet some new friends.	
likes to do grammar exercises.	
likes to go swimming.	
likes to play volleyball.	
needs to go shopping today.	
plans to do winter sports this winter.	
would like to go to the museum today.	
would like to visit New York City.	
would like to go to a concert this weekend.	
is learning to drive.	

SPEAKING ACTIVITY 4

Work in groups of four. Ask each other the questions below. What are the similarities and differences among you? Report to the class about your group.

Names	What do you plan to do when you finish the English program?	What famous place would you like to visit someday?	What famous person would you like to meet?	What do you hope to do in your life?

Grammar Note: Verbs Followed by either Infinitives or Gerunds

Some verbs can be followed by infinitives or by gerunds.

Some of these are *like, love, hate, prefer, begin, start, continue, can't stand.*
Examples:

They love <u>going</u> swimming.   They love <u>to go</u> swimming.

She prefers <u>shopping</u> online.   She prefers <u>to shop</u> online.

Jennifer begins <u>crying</u> when   Jennifer begins <u>to cry</u> when
she's confused.   she's confused.

SPEAKING ACTIVITY 5

Work with a partner. Look at the list of hobbies and pastimes under the chart. Discuss and organize them into the following categories:

Activities We Love Doing	Activities We Dislike Doing	Activities We Would Like to Learn to Do

sewing	going canoeing	going horseback riding
knitting	going camping	playing Ping-Pong
drawing	going shopping	playing video games
collecting coins or stamps	going hiking	working out
going mountain climbing	going skating	going skiing
going bowling	swimming	playing basketball
going fishing	skateboarding	taking pictures and videos

Grammar Note: Verbs Followed by an Object + an Infinitive

Some verbs can take objects + infinitives.

Examples:

The counsellor wants the students to get better marks.

She is teaching them to improve their study skills.

She is asking them to plan their study schedules.

She is telling the students not to eat junk food.

SPEAKING ACTIVITY 6

Make a quick chart with the headings shown on the next page. Walk around the room and ask your classmates these questions. Report the most interesting answers to the class.

What do you want the teacher of this class to do?

What do you want your classmates to do?

What would you like your friends to do?

Name	Teacher	Classmates	Friends

Write about two classmates.

SPEAKING ACTIVITY 7

Complete these sentences by yourself. Then share your answers with a group.

What is the same and what is different about you?

1. My parents often ask me _____.
2. My father always tells me _____.
3. My best friend would like _____.
4. I am teaching myself _____.
5. I don't want my teacher _____.
6. My friends don't want _____.
7. I don't want my classmates _____.
8. I would like this school _____.

LISTENING 1

Before You Listen

PRE-LISTENING ACTIVITY 1

Work with a partner. Who are the people in these photos? What do you know about them?

Look at the list of celebrities and professions below. Match the celebrities and the professions. Check off the celebrities you would like to meet.

Celebrity	Profession *Jobs*
Taylor Swift	*singer*
Brad Pitt	*actor*
Lady Gaga	*singer actor*
Jackie Chan	*martal artist star*
Rafael Nadal	*tennis player*
Prince William	*prince of United Kingdom*
Lionel Messi	*soccer player*
Bill Gates	*Inventor and business man*
Selena Gomez	*actor*

actor	soccer player
singer	martial arts star
prince of United Kingdom	artist
tennis player	inventor and business man

PRE-LISTENING ACTIVITY 2

Make a quick chart with the headings shown below. Work in groups of three. Tell each other who your favourite celebrity is and what you think he or she enjoys doing in his or her free time.

Name	Favourite Celebrity	What the Celebrity Enjoys Doing

PRE-LISTENING VOCABULARY

A. You will hear a conversation on the audio CD that includes the words in the list on the next page. Work with a partner or by yourself to find the definition of each word.

celebrity	fabulous	fan	hobby	charity	to donate
spare *repuesto*	famous	award *otorgar un premio*	facts *hechos*	gift	incredible
movie star	community				

Definitions	Vocabulary
1. more than needed, extra	**spare**
2. a free-time activity	hobby
3. an organization that gives food, money, or help to those who need it	charity
4. to give	to donate
5. a group of people	community
6. someone who admires and looks up to a famous person = movie start	fan
7. true information	facts
8. a well-known actor who stars in films	movie star
9. unbelievable, something hard to believe	incredible
10. a present	gift
11. well known (person = celebrity)	famous
12. a prize → un premio	an award
13. a person everyone knows about; a famous person	celebrity
14. excellent, wonderful	faboulos / incredible

Listening STRATEGY 🎧
Use the context and the vocabulary you know to help you understand the meaning.

B. Choose the correct words from the list to fill in the blanks in these sentences. Use each word only once. Not all the words are used in the sentences.

1. Many celebrities ___donate___ money to ___charity / charities___.

2. Taylor Swift is a ___celebrity___ in country music. She gave a ___gift / donnation___ of $4,000,000 to the Country Music Hall of Fame and Museum.

3. Bill Gates is ___famous___ all over the world.

4. My ___hobby___ is taking pictures.

5. Brad Pitt has thousands of ___fans___. They think he's wonderful.

6. What a ___famous / clothing___ outfit. You look great in it.

7. Brad Pitt works with UNICEF (the United Nations International Children's Emergency fund). He's an ___incredible___ person.

8. She does volunteer work to help the people in the ___community___.

9. Do you have any ___facts___ about that charity?

10. Taylor Swift wins many ___awards___ for her singing.

Listening for the Main Ideas

Listen to the conversation and answer the questions.

 **Track 35**

1. What is the conversation between Natasha and Janice about?
2. Why are they talking about this topic? *Lobby*
3. What is the relationship between Natasha and Janice? *friends*

Listening Comprehension

Listen to the conversation as many times as necessary. Write *T* if the statement is true or *F* if it is false.

 **Track 36**

1. Janice likes Natasha's jacket and her haircut. *T*
2. Natasha often reads about movie stars and singers on the Internet. *T*
3. Selena Gomez can't stand chocolate. *F*
4. Selena Gomez dislikes playing sports. *F*
5. Taylor Swift and Selena Gomez don't know each other. *T*
6. Taylor Swift doesn't do very much charity work. *F*
7. Taylor Swift loves playing with her cat. *T*
8. Brad Pitt doesn't help children's charities. *F*
9. Janice and Natasha dislike the stars for their charity work. *F*
10. Janice and Natasha plan to have coffee the next day. *F*

Personalizing

A. Work in groups of four. Tell each other who your role model is. Describe your role model's special qualities. Explain why you want to be like this person.

Names	Role Models	Descriptions	Reasons

B. Work with a partner and discuss these questions.

1. How much spare time do you usually have during the week?
2. What do you usually do in your spare time?

3. What other things would you like to do in your spare time? Why?

4. Some people say we should do the following things in our free time. Which ones do you agree with?
   a. make a plan and don't waste your spare time
   b. don't do anything stressful
   c. learn new things
   d. spend time with pets
   e. spend time with friends

5. What is the best way to spend free time, in your opinion?

Vocabulary and Language Chunks

Write the number of the expression next to the meaning. After checking your answers choose five expressions and write your own sentences.

Words and Expressions	**Meanings**
1. to look great	_8_ to meet friends or family
2. to have good taste	_6_ free time
3. to find out *descubrir*	_1_ to look very nice
4. to hang out *salir*	_9_ to get ready to leave or to do something
5. to go to concerts	_7_ someone people admire and try to be like
6. spare time	_3_ to learn information
7. role model *modelo a seguir*	_2_ to know what looks fashionable or attractive
8. to get together	_4_ to spend time with someone, not doing anything special
9. to get going	_5_ to attend concerts

SPEAKING 2

Communication Focus 2:
Starting and Closing Conversations

When we want to start a conversation we can use some of the following structures:

Structures/Expressions	Examples	Responses
How's it going? How are you doing?	Hey, John! How's it going?	Just great! What about you?
What's new? What's up? What are you up to these days?	Hi, Allen. What's up?	Not too much. I'm studying for final exams. What are you up to?
You look great. I like (love) your _____.	Hi, Monica. You look nice! I love that colour on you.	Thanks. Blue is my favourite colour.
Your _____ looks nice. Your _____ is fantastic.	Your sweater is fantastic.	Thanks. It was a present from my sister. Your sweater is really nice too.
Your _____ looks terrific. Your _____ is great.	Your jacket looks terrific on you. Fred, your English is great.	Thanks.
What do you think of . . .?	Hi, George! What do you think of the new class schedules?	I'm not crazy about starting classes at 8:00 AM, but I like finishing early on Fridays.

One way that people show they want to start a conversation is by complimenting a person's clothing or ability. After this, a conversation about another topic can begin.

Another good way to start a conversation is to ask open-ended questions such as "What do you think of. . .?" "How do you feel about . . .?"

Opening with a compliment and then continuing with an open-ended question is a good way to begin a conversation. Relaxed, open body language shows that people are ready to start a conversation.

When we want to end a conversation we can use some of these structures and expressions:

Structures/Expressions	Examples	Responses
I have to go now. It was good (nice/great) talking to you.	Well, Ann, I have to go now. It was good talking to you.	Yeah. Talk to you soon.
Sorry I can't talk longer. I need to . . .	Sorry I can't talk longer, Mark. I need to finish my presentation for tomorrow's class.	Good luck with it. See you soon.
Anyway, gotta (I've got to) go . . .	Anyway Tony, I gotta go. I'm meeting a friend at the coffee shop.	Okay. Have a good one.
Okay, then. I need to . . .	Okay, then. Well, I need to finish my shopping. Good talking to you.	Nice talking to you too.

When people want to end a conversation they often use body language such as standing up, packing up books, putting on a coat, or looking away.

SPEAKING ACTIVITY 8

Form two concentric circles. Face the students in the other circle.

The teacher will choose a conversation topic. When the teacher gives a signal such as clapping his or her hands, greet the person opposite you and start a conversation. Continue talking until the teacher gives the signal to stop. End the conversation.

Then one circle moves clockwise while the other circle moves counter-clockwise until the teacher gives the signal to stop.

The teacher will then give you another topic. Start another conversation with the person facing you, until the teacher gives the signal to stop. End the conversation, and continue moving in circles and starting and stopping conversations until the teacher tells you to end this activity.

Report about the most interesting conversation you had.

Topics for Conversation

the weather	favourite entertainer	your favourite food
our classroom	your favourite sport	favourite holiday
our school	favourite way of spending free time	dream job
this city	last weekend/summer/vacation	plans after this course

Communication Focus 3: Giving Instructions

When we give instructions, we use commands and sequence words to tell the order in which to do actions.

Structures/Expressions	Examples
First, . . .	**First, open** the washing machine door.
Then . . . Next . . .	**Then, put** the clothes into the machine. **Next, choose** the water temperature.
After that . . .	**After that, add** the detergent. **Then choose** the normal or delicate washing cycle.
Finally, . . . Last, . . .	**Finally, press** the start button. **Last, press** the start button.

 SPEAKING ACTIVITY 9

A. Work with a partner. Read the instructions for making toast on the next page. The instructions are out of order.

Instructions for Making Toast

Take the toast out.

Start the toaster.

Could you please tell me how to use the toaster?

Put the bread into the toaster.

Wait a few minutes until the toast pops up.

Take the toaster out of the cupboard.

Below are the instructions placed in the correct order to make a dialogue. Practise the dialogue together.

Dialogue

Person A: Could you please tell me how to use the toaster?

Person B: Sure. First take the toaster out of the cupboard.

Person A: Okay, then what do I do?

Person B: Then put the bread into the toaster. After that, start the toaster.

Person A: What's next?

Person B: Wait a few minutes until the toast pops up.

Finally, take the toast out.

B. Make a dialogue for each task below. Put the instructions into the correct order and use commands and sequence words as in the sample dialogue. Practise saying your dialogues. After that, make up your own dialogue and say it for the class.

Instructions for Making Green Tea

Serve the tea.

Fill the teapot with boiling water.

Take the teapot out of the cupboard.

Boil some water.

Wait a few minutes.

Put the tea leaves into the teapot.

Could you please show me how to make tea?

Instructions for Changing a Light Bulb

Screw the new light bulb into the socket.

Turn on the light.

Turn off the light.

Could you please teach me how to change the light bulb?

Get a new light bulb.

Unscrew the old light bulb from the socket.

Communication Focus 4: Making General Requests

English speakers make requests in different ways. The form of the request depends on the situation and how formal it is, and how serious the request is.

	Structure	Example Sentence	Sample Response
More Formal	*Would you mind . . . +* gerund	Would you mind opening the door?	Of course not. I'll do it right now.
	Would you please . . .	Would you please open the door?	Of course.
	Could you please . . .	Could you please open the door?	Certainly.
Less Formal	*Would you . . .*	Would you open the door?	Sure.
	Could you . . .	Could you open the door?	No problem.
	Can you . . .	Can you open the door?	Okay.
Direct Command	base form of the verb	Open the door	Okay.
	want + object + infinitive/ *would like* + object + infinitive	I want you to open the door. I would like you to open the door.	All right.

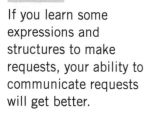

SPEAKING ACTIVITY 10

Speaking STRATEGY

If you learn some expressions and structures to make requests, your ability to communicate requests will get better.

A. Work with a partner. Read the dialogue sentences below. Put the dialogue in order and then practise it with your partner.

Person A: I see. Well, could you come and get me when your meeting is over?

Person B: Sure, no problem. I'm leaving in a couple of minutes.

Person B: No, sorry. I have a meeting that starts at 3:30.

Person A: Could you pick me up after school, too? I finish at 3:30.

Person B: All right.

Person A: Could you please give me a lift to class? I'm really late.

B. With your partner, make up a dialogue to go with each picture below. Present your dialogues to the class.

SPEAKING ACTIVITY 11

Work with a partner. Talk about some requests you would like to make in these places.

At School	At Home	Other Place: _____
_____	_____	_____
_____	_____	_____
_____	_____	_____

LISTENING 2

Before You Listen

PRE-LISTENING ACTIVITY 1

Work with a partner. What is happening in these pictures? What is your opinion of what the students are doing?

PRE-LISTENING ACTIVITY 2

Work with a partner. You are going to listen to an information session on the audio CD about studying for tests. Predict three things that you think the speaker will say.

1. _I think she reads and listening to music, she is concentrating_
2. _they look the information and they study, really interesting_
3. _I think he worked a lot now he sleeps_

Listening STRATEGY

If you try to prepare for what you are going to hear, this will help you understand the listening.

PRE-LISTENING VOCABULARY

A. You will hear a conversation on the audio CD that includes the following words. Work with a partner or by yourself to find the definition of each word.

success	to review	to cram *abarrotar*	space	
energy	brain	diagram	*visual* visual aid *ayuda*	grade
to challenge *desafiar*	concentration	regulations	session	

Definitions	Vocabulary
1. to look over, to study again	**to review**
2. to learn a lot of information in a short time, to completely fill up	to cram
3. area available for a certain purpose	space
4. drawing, sketch, picture, or chart , a diagram, table	diagram
5. something you can see which helps you learn	visual aid
6. to compete against, have a contest with someone	to challenge
7. putting all your attention on one thing	concentration
8. the organ in the head that controls thoughts, feelings, and actions	brain
9. the strength to do physical or mental activities	energy
10. mark, score	grade
11. a period of time used for a special purpose, such as a class or a meeting	session
12. rules	regulation
13. reaching and accomplishing a goal	success

B. Choose the correct words from the list to fill in the blanks in these sentences. Use each word only once. Not all the words are used in the sentences. Please make changes to the verbs or nouns if necessary.

1. You need to ___review___ your notes before the grammar test.

2. The teacher wants _to challenge_ the students to get better ___grades___ on the next test.

3. It's not a good idea ___to cram___ for tests and exams because you won't remember very much.

4. The professor used pictures or _visual aids_ to help the students understand the vocabulary.

5. Eating healthy food gives you ___energy___.

6. He drew a ___diagram___ of all the verb tenses.

7. Let's go to the library to study. There's a lot of ___space___ there for us to work.

8. He can speak four languages. He has a lot of ___success___ in learning languages.

9. Students need to find out all the rules and ___regulations___ before the exam.

Listening for the Main Ideas

Track 37   Listen to the information session and answer the questions.

1. Who is the speaker?

2. Who is listening to the information? *students*

3. Why is the speaker giving the information session? *exam preparation - her job is to give tips to students*

4. What does the speaker hope? *can better grades and organize to study tempos*

Listening Comprehension

Listen to the information session as many times as necessary. Label the activities as good or bad ideas when studying for tests.

 **Track 38**

1. Studying at the last minute _____is a bad idea_____. *cramming, to cram*

2. Giving yourself enough time to study _____is a good idea_____.

3. Planning your study schedule _____is a good idea_____.

4. Cramming _____is bad idea_____. *atesfar*

5. Studying for two or more tests during the same time period
_____is a good idea_____.

6. Having computer games and cellphones when you study
_____is a bad idea_____.

7. Studying at a comfortable desk and chair _____is a good idea_____.

8. Having enough light _____is a good idea_____.

9. Making diagrams and charts _____is a good idea_____. *visual ideas*

10. Doing practice tests _____is a good idea_____.

11. Having fun with friends during study groups _____is a bad idea_____.

12. Studying for many hours without stopping _____is a bad idea_____.

13. Eating junk food _____is bad idea_____.

14. Drinking water _____is a good idea_____.

15. Rushing on exam day _____is a bad idea_____.

Personalizing

Make a quick chart with the headings shown below. Work with a small group. Make a list of the best ways to do the following. Share your answers with the class.

The Best Ways to Get Good Marks	The Best Ways to Learn a New Language	The Best Ways to Meet New People	The Best Ways to Spend Free Time
playing your schedule	learning 10 words×d	online, at the party	reade a book
doing practice test	watching the english movi and listen to music.	party	dancing, gardening
making diagrams and chats			walking, watch theTV etc

Vocabulary and Language Chunks

Write the number of the expression next to the meaning. After checking your answers, choose five expressions and write your own sentences.

Words and Expressions

1. to put away *ponto frenv*
2. to make sure *osegurarse*
3. practice makes perfect *hace to perfeciòn*
4. at the last minute *ultimo momento*
5. to get to *para llegar o*
6. to focus on *concentrarse en*
7. plenty of *mucho*
8. to give someone a tip
9. to set up *configurar*

Meanings

___9___ to arrange, to organize

___8___ to give someone special information

___5___ to arrive at   *llegar o*

___7___ a lot of

___6___ to pay attention to, concentrate on

___1___ to put in another place

___2___ to check and be sure about

___3___ doing something many times makes you better at it

___4___ at the latest possible time

PRONUNCIATION

Pronunciation Focus 1: Unstressed Vowels—The Schwa

 PRONUNCIATION ACTIVITY 1

Track 39

A. Listen to the underlined vowels in the pairs of words in Column A and Column B. Do they sound the same? Write *yes* or *no*.

Column A	Column B	Same Sound?
m<u>a</u>n	repairm<u>a</u>n	_____
l<u>a</u>nd	Scotl<u>a</u>nd	_____
l<u>e</u>ss	usel<u>e</u>ss	_____
f<u>u</u>ll	caref<u>u</u>l	_____
b<u>a</u>nd	husb<u>a</u>nd	_____

The underlined vowels in Column B don't sound the same as those in Column A. The vowels in Column B are not stressed. English speakers pronounce unstressed vowels as a schwa. The schwa sounds like / uh /. For example, in the word *Canada*, the second two vowels are schwas.

B. Listen to each word and then repeat.

breakfast   famous   England   woman   model   concert

soccer   jacket   ticket   kitchen   apple   tennis

C. How many syllables are there in each word? Which syllable is stressed? Which vowel is pronounced as a schwa?

In English nouns of two syllables we usually stress the vowel in the first syllable and we pronounce the vowel in the second syllable as a schwa. This happens 90 percent of the time.

PRONUNCIATION ACTIVITY 2

A. Listen to these words. Cross out each vowel pronounced as a schwa.  **Track 40**

1. Can~~a~~d~~a~~
2. banana
3. cabbage
4. salad
5. excellent
6. language
7. success
8. schedule
9. beautiful
10. photography
11. concert
12. famous
13. compliment

B. Work with a partner to practise saying the words.

C. Make up five sentences with these words and practise saying them.

PRONUNCIATION ACTIVITY 3

When words end with *-er* or *-ian*, the vowel in this syllable is pronounced as a schwa.  **Track 41**

A. Listen to these words and underline the unstressed syllable.

1. actor
2. singer
3. dancer
4. musician
5. doctor
6. teacher
7. firefighter
8. librarian
9. designer
10. player
11. inventor
12. technician

B. Work with a partner to practise saying the words.

C. Make up five sentences with these words.

PRONUNCIATION ACTIVITY 4

A. Listen to these words. Write each word in the Adjective column when you hear it. **Track 42**

Adjective	Opposite	Adjective	Opposite
1.		9.	
2.		10.	
3.		11.	
4.		12.	
5.		13.	
6.		14.	
7.		15.	
8.		16.	

B. Work with a partner and write the opposites of the adjectives.

C. Practise saying the words to your partner. Then, make five sentences with some of the words and present them to the class.

 **PRONUNCIATION ACTIVITY 5**

A. Work with a partner. Compare the occupations below. Which occupations have a better salary, and which are more interesting? Which are easier or more difficult? Which are more fun?

B. Make five comparisons and present your ideas to the class.

dentist	graphic artist	flight attendant
pilot	teacher	hotel manager
video-game designer	family physician	librarian
nurse	lawyer	personal trainer
chef	police officer	magician

Pronunciation Focus 2: Intonation with *Yes/No* Questions

When English speakers ask questions which can be answered with *Yes* or *No*, the voice rises on the last important word in the sentence.
Examples:

↗
Are you tired?   Can I leave early? ↗

PRONUNCIATION ACTIVITY 6

Track 43

A. Work with a partner. In the sentences below draw rising arrows on the words where you think the voice goes up or rises.
Example:
↗
Are you okay?

1. Can I help?
2. Would you open the door?
3. Can you lend me $10?
4. Is she hungry?
5. Could I borrow some sugar?
6. Would you please close the door?
7. When are you leaving?
8. Could you pick me up after class?
9. Can I give you a lift?

10. What time is it?
11. Do you live nearby?
12. Do they want me to come early?
13. Where are you from?
14. Are these your books?
15. What are you doing?
16. Do you like action movies?
17. Do they want to go camping?
18. Does he live downtown?

B. Listen to the sentences and check your answers.

C. Practise saying the sentences to your partner.

👥 **PRONUNCIATION ACTIVITY 7**

Work with a partner. Make *Yes/No* questions for the following answers.
Then practise saying the dialogues.

Examples:

Answer: No, Ann hates
bowling.

Question: <u>Does Ann like going bowling?</u>

Answer: No, you can't.

Question: <u>Can we leave early today?</u>

1. _____

No, it isn't.

2. _____

Yes. They're very happy.

3. _____

I'm sorry, I don't have any money.

4. _____

It's a quarter to three.

5. _____

No, I can't stand shrimp.

6. _____

No, I actually prefer staying home on Saturday nights.

7. _____

Sure. I'm not using it right now.

8. _____

Okay, but I don't like Chinese food as much as Japanese food.

9. _____

No, they don't. My mother lives in Hong Kong and my father lives
in Montreal.

10. _____

Yes. I love it when you cook supper.

11. _____

Yes, could you please bring me these shoes in size 9.

12. _____

I'm sorry, I can't. My notes are at home.

COMMUNICATING IN THE REAL WORLD

A. Use your English to talk to people outside your classroom. On your own or with a partner, talk to five people outside your class. Ask them the questions below and record the information. Make a short report to the class about what you learned.

Before you begin, say this:

> May I ask you some questions? This is an assignment for my English class.

1. Who is your favourite celebrity? What is his/her profession?— singer, actor, or _____? Why do you like him/her?

2. What do you like doing in your free time in the evenings?

3. What do you enjoy doing in the winter?

4. What famous place would you like to visit?

5. What famous person would you like to meet?

B. Project: Work with a partner or small group. Do some research to find out information about a celebrity or famous person you all admire. Find out about this person's life and achievements. You may find your information in current magazines or on the Internet. Your teacher will give you some suggestions.

Make a presentation to the class.

SELF-EVALUATION

Think about your work in this chapter. For each row in the chart sections Grammar and Language Functions, Learning Strategies, and Pronunciation, give yourself a score based on the rating scale below and write a comment in the Notes section.

Show the chart to your teacher. Talk about what you need to do to make your English better.

Rating Scale

1	2	3	4	5

Needs improvement. ←————————————————————→ *Great!*

	Score	Notes
Grammar and Language Functions		
talking about entertainment and free time activities		
using infinitives and gerunds		
understanding and talking about likes and dislikes		
starting and ending conversations		
giving and understanding instructions		
understanding and making requests		
Pronunciation		
recognizing and pronouncing unstressed vowels		
recognizing and using correct intonation in *Yes/No* questions		
Learning Strategies		
Speaking		
using the expressions and structures for making requests so that I can communicate better		
Listening		
using the context of the listening and the vocabulary I know to help myself understand		
preparing for what I am going to listen to, to help myself understand what I am hearing		

Vocabulary and Language Chunks
Look at this list of new vocabulary and language chunks you learned in this chapter. Give yourself a score based on the rating scale and write a comment.

to put away	to focus on	to look great
to go to concerts	to make sure	plenty of
to have good taste	spare time	practice makes perfect
to give someone a tip	find out	to get going
at the last minute	to set up	to be up to
role model	enough time	to hang out
to get together		

	Score	Notes
understanding new vocabulary and language chunks		
using new words and phrases correctly		

Write six sentences and use new vocabulary you learned in this chapter.

1. _____
2. _____
3. _____
4. _____
5. _____
6. _____

My plan for practising is _____

_____

_____

_____

_____

CHAPTER 5

You Are What You Eat

Food and Experiences

- Talking about completed actions
- Telling a story about the past
- Making excuses and giving explanations
- Talking about actions in progress at specific times in the past

THINKING AND TALKING

Make up a title for each picture and then complete the questionnaire on your own. Work with a partner and compare your answers. Report to the class about the differences between you and your partner.

Questionnaire

Put a check mark next to the foods you like to eat. How often do you usually eat these foods?

Foods	Like or Dislike?	How Often?
pizza	like	rarely
hot dogs/hamburgers	dislike	
salad	like	every day
rice	like	sometimes
bread	like	sometimes
candy	dislike	sometime
chocolate	like	rarely
fast food/junk food	dislike	
fruit	like	every day
vegetables	like	always
meat	like	3 times a week
fish/seafood	like	4 times a week
cakes/desserts	like	rarely
snacks	like	rarely
other: oatmeal,milk.	like	always

ᴀ̊ᴀ̊ SPEAKING ACTIVITY 1

Work with a partner. Put the foods in the list on the next page into the correct categories in the chart. You can also add other foods not on this list.

chicken ✓   fish ✓   apples ✓   oranges ✓
pastries   olives ✓   lettuce ✓   couscous
noodles ✓   hot dogs ✓   rice   soup ✓
lamb   beef ✓   shrimp ✓   turkey ✓
stew ✓   ice cream   cake ✓   pie ✓
berengena   eggplant ✓   plums ✓   tomatoes ✓   sausage *salchichas*
calamar   squid ✓   pork ✓   pizza ✓   beans *frijoles*
corn ✓   peppers   spices   seaweed *algas marinas*
honey ✓   sushi ✓   salad ✓   potato chips

Fruit	Vegetables	Meat	Fish and Seafood	Other
apples	olives	chicken	fish	pastries
oranges	lettuce	lamb	shrimp	couscous
plums	eggplant	beef	squid	noodles
	tomatoes	turkey	seaweed	ice cream
	beans	sausage	sushi	rice
	corn	pork		soup
	peppers	stew		honey
	salad	hot dogs		spices
	potato			cake
				pie
				sausage
				pizza
				beans

Grammar Note: Count/Mass Nouns

English nouns can be count (countable) or mass (uncountable).
Countable nouns have a singular and a plural form. Verb agreement can
be singular or plural.

Uncountable nouns do not have a plural form.

	Countable Nouns	Uncountable Nouns
Singular	A banana is a good snack.	Coffee is a strong drink.
Plural	Bananas are good snacks.	

These categories of nouns are usually uncountable:

Categories	Examples
liquids	coffee, tea, juice, water, soda pop, paint, oil, perfume
small granular things	rice, sugar, salt, pepper, flour, sand, dust
materials	gold, silver, wood, steel, metal, wool, cotton, glass
gases	air, pollution
some categories of food*	meat, seafood, cheese, bread, fruit

*Sometimes these foods are used in the plural, but then they mean "kinds of" or "varieties of." For example, the *cheeses of France* means the kinds of cheese in France.

Other common nouns which are uncountable are *time, money, furniture, hair,* and *weather,* and abstract nouns such as *love, homework, health,* and *happiness.*

We use *many* or *a few* with countable nouns.

We use *much* or *a little* with uncountable nouns. Verb agreement is singular.

much/many	How **many** bananas are there?	How **much** coffee is there?
a few/a little	There are **a few** bananas.	There is **a little** coffee.
a lot of	There are **a lot of** bananas.	There is **a lot of** coffee.

SPEAKING ACTIVITY 2

Make up eight questions about food using *much* or *many*. Use the lists of food above or any other food in your questions. Interview three people in your class, ask these questions, and record their answers. When you are answering questions, try to give as much information as you can. Report to the class about the most unusual answers.

Questions	Interviewee 1	Interviewee 2	Interviewee 3
Example: How much ice cream do you eat?	Not too much in the winter, but I eat a lot of ice cream in the summer.	I eat a little ice cream. I like it but it's fattening so I try not to eat a lot.	I eat a lot of ice cream. I enjoy eating ice cream.
1. How many bottle of water do you drink every day.			
2. How much money do you spend for food par week?			
3. How many hours do you walk par day?			
4. How much milk do you put in your coffee?			
5. How much food do you eat par day?			
6. How many canes of juice do you want?			
7. How many friends that your daughter have?			
8. How many shoes do you have?			

ⁿⁿ SPEAKING ACTIVITY 3

Answer the questions. Then work with a partner and ask him or her the questions. Report to the class about the most interesting information you learned.

Question	Me	My Partner *Leila*
1. What is your favourite meat?	*my favourite meat is pork*	*beef*
2. What is your favourite seafood?	*my favourite seafood is fish*	*fish*
3. What is your favourite vegetable?	*my favourite vegetable is carrot*	*carrot*
4. What is your favourite fruit?	*my favourite fruit is guayaba*	*water melon*
5. What is your favourite dessert?	*my favourite dessert is dulce de leche*	*marmud*
6. What is your favourite snack?	*my favourite snack is tostitos*	*Jheto9.*
7. What is your favourite drink?	*my favourite drink is coffee.*	*Coffe and coone.*

Leila's favourite meat is beef.

Saimous's favourite seafood is fish.

SPEAKING 1

Communication Focus 1:
Talking about Completed Actions

We use the simple past tense to talk about completed actions in the past.
Examples:

> The teacher arrived a few minutes ago.

> She asked the students to open their books.

Grammar Note: Simple Past Tense

We form the simple past of regular verbs by adding -*ed* to the verb stem. Most verbs in English are regular. These are the forms of the simple past tense.

Affirmative	Negative	Interrogative
they cooked	they didn't cook	Did they cook?
she travelled	she didn't travel	Did she travel?
we shouted	we didn't shout	Did we shout?

We use the past tense with these time expressions.

last night	**yesterday**	two hours **ago**
last year	**before**	a few weeks **ago**
last week	**at that time**	many years **ago**

Pronunciation Note

The regular past tense ending -ed can be pronounced in three different ways.

Pronounce the -ed as /əd/ when the verb stem ends in /t/ or /d/. (Note: This adds a syllable to the verb.)	Pronounce the -ed as /t/ when the verb stem ends in a voiceless consonant sound— /p/, /f/, /sh/, /ch/, /k/, /s/ (Note: This does not add a syllable to the verb.)	Pronounce the -ed as /d/ when the verb stem ends in a voiced consonant sound. (Note: This does not add a syllable to the verb.)
We started.	He laughed.	They served. _Zert_
She invited.	They cooked.	She listened. _lizent_
They landed.	I danced.	We answered. _anzert_

 PRONUNCIATION ACTIVITY 1

Work with a partner and write the past tense of these verbs. Then put the verbs into the correct boxes according to the pronunciation of the past tense ending. Finally, make up five sentences using the past tense of some of these verbs.

visit _ed_　try _ied_　push _ed_　seat _ed_
wash _ed_　study _ied_　complete _d_　look _ed_
watch _ed_　decide _d_　need _ed_　sound _ed_
shop _ped_　describe _d_　use _d_　push _ed_

-ed pronounced as /t/	-ed pronounced as /d/	-ed pronounced as /əd/
washed	used	visited
watched	tried	dicided
looked	studied	needed
shopped	described	seated
pushed		sounded
		completed

Speaking STRATEGY

Paying attention to verb forms and using the correct tense helps other people understand the time when events happened.

SPEAKING ACTIVITY 4

Walk around the room and talk to six classmates. Find out and record the answers to these questions. Report to the class about two of your partners. Use complete sentences.

Roghad 6/wdys

Question	Partner 1	Partner 2	Partner 3	Partner 4	Partner 5	Partner 6
When did you last invite someone to visit you?	she invited her friend last week	last weekedo				
What food or drink did you serve your guest?	she served pizza and coke	she serve tomate with soup rice				
Did you have a good time? Explain why.	yes had a good time she had a good time because she takes to much talk with her fried	yes enjoys she enjoy the week because they not see				

👥 SPEAKING ACTIVITY 5

Work with a partner. Find out the answers to these questions and report the most interesting information to the class.

Questions	Answers
1. When did you last cook or bake something? What was it? Did you like it?	
2. When did you last order take-out food? What was it? How did you like it?	
3. When did you last eat in a restaurant? Did you like it? How much did you tip the server?	
4. When did you last ask for a recipe? What recipe was it?	
5. When did you last shop for food? Where did you go? What did you buy?	

👥 SPEAKING ACTIVITY 6

Make a quick chart with the headings shown below. Work in groups of three. Tell each other four things you did and four things you didn't do last week. Then ask each other about four other actions. Report the most interesting answers to the class.

Name	What did you do last week?	What didn't you do last week?	Did you go shopping?
Hanelle	I studied English. I visited my daughter.	I didn't go shopping I didn't bought the groceries	yes, I did go to the park. No, I didn't go to the park.

Communication Focus 2: Telling a Story about the Past

When we tell a story about the past, we use the following words and expressions to explain the order of the actions.

Structure	Examples
first/first of all/	**First** I washed
then/next/after that/	**Then** I dressed. **Next** I cooked breakfast. **After that** I ate breakfast and looked at the newspaper.
finally	**Finally** I was ready for school.

👥 SPEAKING ACTIVITY 7

Work with a partner. Talk about four things you did yesterday morning. Use *first, then, after that,* and *finally*. Then talk about what you did yesterday evening. First one partner tells about himself or herself. Then the other partner tells what he or she did. You can use some of these verbs. (Remember to use the pronunciation rules for the regular past tense.)

Morning Actions	Evening Actions
brush	study
wash	call
comb	watch
dress	cook
listen	clean
cook	talk
clean	play
walk	chat

Me

Yesterday Morning	Yesterday Evening

My Partner

Yesterday Morning	Yesterday Evening

SPEAKING ACTIVITY 8

Listening STRATEGY

A. Make a quick chart with the headings shown below. Walk around the room and speak to eight classmates. Ask these questions. Report to the class.

Listening for time expressions such as *first*, *next*, and *after that* helps you understand the order in which events happened.

1. Where did you live five years ago?

2. When did you arrive here?

3. What did you do first?

4. What did you do next?

5. What did you do after that?

Name	Previous Residence	Date of Arrival	First Action	Next Action	Next Action

B. Write about two students.

 SPEAKING ACTIVITY 9

Work with a partner to read this story and underline the verbs. Then retell the story about last year. Use the past tense. Read the story out loud to your partner.

Mary Ann's Seafood Palace

Tony is a server. He works at Mary Ann's Seafood Palace, a friendly neighbourhood restaurant in San Diego, California. Tony lives in California because he doesn't like cold weather and he hates the snow and ice and freezing temperatures in places like Canada. Tony doesn't have a perfect life but he's happy. He works from early morning until late at night.

First thing in the morning, Tony helps Mary Ann shop for food at the markets. They look for fresh seafood and vegetables. Then Mary Ann plans the menu. After that, she cooks the daily specials and she often bakes pies and cakes too. Mary Ann changes the menu every day.

The Seafood Palace opens at lunchtime. Tony helps Mary Ann welcome the customers. Some customers arrive early because the restaurant is popular, and they often need to line up to get a table. They love the food and they order a lot of it. Tony works hard and the customers tip him very well. Tony and Mary Ann always talk and laugh with the customers. They enjoy their work, but they need to close the restaurant because Mary Ann wants to travel more and Tony wants to go back to school.

Last year, Tony was a server _____

_____

_____

👥 SPEAKING ACTIVITY 10

Read the biography of Justin Bieber. Then, work with a partner and fill in the chart. After that, fill in the chart about each other and make a short presentation to the class about your partner's biography.

Justin Bieber was born on March 1, 1994. He was born in Stratford, a small town in Ontario. He attended school in Stratford and lived with his mother. She helped him develop his musical ability. Then when he was 12 years old, he entered a singing contest. He finished second in the contest. His mother was very proud of him. After that, she started to put videos of Justin singing on YouTube for other people in the family to see. Many people all over the world watched Justin's videos. His fans wanted to see and hear more about Justin. In just two years he was a success and a superstar. He produced and recorded many hit songs and signed a record deal.

Fact Sheet on Justin Bieber

Place of birth (Where was he born?)	He was born in Stratford a small town in Ontar
Date of birth (When was he born?)	He was
Where did he attend school?	
Who did he live with?	
What did he do as a 12-year-old?	
What happened after that?	
What happened next?	
What happened then?	

Fact Sheet on My Partner _Autography_

Place of birth	I was born in guajira Colombia
Date of birth	I was born on Jun 8, 1968
Where my partner attended school	I atted school in Ocaña Colombia
Who my partner lived with	I lived with my mom my granmother and my aunt for
One interesting thing my partner did as a teenager	at a teenager I played basketball very well and I play for represent my school every year.

What happened after that	*when my husband was killed I moved to canada with my children and my mother; I had gift for M*
What happened next	*when I arrived to Quebec and lerned French I star a business and I had gift for M*
What happened then	

Grammar Note: Irregular Verbs

In English, 97 percent of all verbs are regular, but there are some very important irregular verbs which we use very often. The eight most common English verbs are irregular. They are the verbs *to be, to have, to do, to go, to say, to see, to take,* and *to get.**

These are the past tense forms of some irregular verbs:

Affirmative	Question Form	With Question Words
she had	Did she have . . .?	What did she have?
they did	Did they do . . .?	What did they do?
we went	Did we go . . .?	Why did we go?
I said	Did I say . . .?	When did I say?
he took	Did he take . . .?	When did he take?
you saw	Did you see . . .?	What did you see?
they got	Did they get . . .?	What did they get?

Negative	Contractions
she did not have	she didn't have
they did not do	they didn't do
we did not go	we didn't go
I did not say	I didn't say
he did not take	he didn't take
you did not see	you didn't see
they did not get	they didn't get

*Please see the list of irregular verbs in the Appendix.

SPEAKING ACTIVITY 11

These are the present and past tense forms of some irregular verbs. Use them in the following activity.

go—went	eat—ate	get—got
take—took	do—did	have—had
speak—spoke	see—saw	say—said

A. Work with a partner. Look at the chart on the next page. Answer the questions about yourself and then ask your partner the same questions.

Questions	Me	My Partner
1. When did you last go to a party?	I went to the party	
2. What did you take to the party?	I brought a cake	
3. What interesting food did you eat?	I ate a chicken with champingnos *souce*	
4. What kind of drinks did you have?	I drank a glass of red wine	
5. What did you do at the party?	I danced too much	
6. How many people did you speak to?	I spoke with three people	
7. What did you say to the host? *anfintrion*	I said thank you for invited me	
8. What did you see that was interesting?	I saw a beautiful dress	
9. What time did you get home? *a que horas regaso*	I got home around five Pm	
10. Did you have a good time? Explain why.	Yes, I had a good time because I was my family	

B. Write about your partner's party. Report to the class.

_____

_____

_____

SPEAKING ACTIVITY 12

These are some more irregular verbs in the present and past tenses. Work
with a partner to change the sentences to tell this story in the past tense.
Then tell your partner six things about a course you took, and find out
about a course your partner took.

Hegvour

get—got	read—read	have—had
teach—taught	write—wrote	be—was/were
understand—understood	take—took	spend—spent
speak—spoke	make—made	

Example:

Elizabeth takes a Spanish course on Tuesday evenings.

Last winter Elizabeth took a Spanish course on Tuesday evenings.

1. She gets to school at 7 PM.

   Yesterday she got to school at 7 PM.

2. The teacher teaches until 8 PM.

   Last week the teacher taught until 8 PM

3. Then the class takes a break.

   Then the class took a break.

4. The students speak Spanish during the break.

   The students spoke Spanish during the break.

5. After that, they read Spanish stories.

   After that, they read Spanish stories.

6. Next they write sentences in Spanish.

   Next they wrote sentences in Spanish.

7. Then they take up the sentences and speak to each other.

   Then they took up the sentences and spoke to each other.   *Tooke up → reformation*

8. They spend a lot of time speaking Spanish.

   They spent a lot of time speaking Spanish.

9. They make friends with each other.

   They made friends with each other.

10. The students have a good time in the class.

    The students has a good time in the class.

11. Most of the students understand a lot of Spanish.   *mucho*

    Most of the students understood a lot of Spanish.

12. The class is over at 9:30 and Elizabeth finally gets home at 10:00 PM.

    The class was over at 9:30 and Elizabeth finally got home at 10:00 PM.

The Courses We Took	
Me	**My Partner**

LISTENING 1

Before You Listen

👥 PRE-LISTENING ACTIVITY

A. Look at the pictures below. Work with a partner to decide on a title for each picture. Use one of the following titles, or make up your own title.

abajo

A Meal in Morocco   A Delicious Dinner

A Japanese Family Meal   At a Moroccan Restaurant

Preparing Dinner in Morocco   A Special Meal

A Japanese family meal   *Preparing dinner in Morocco*   *A meal in morocco*   *A special meal*

eating in the floor
eting with their hand

B. What are some differences in eating habits that you see in the pictures?

C. What differences in eating habits are there between your hometown and your current city?   *in my city it is not well seen to eat with your hands*

PRE-LISTENING VOCABULARY

A. You will hear a conversation on the audio CD that includes the following words. Work with a partner or by yourself to find the definition of each word.

spicy	towel *toalla*	adventure	delicious	appetizer	stew *guiso*
server	unusual *inusual*	dessert	fantastic	raw *crudo*	wedding
kneel *arrodillarse*	traditional	cushion *cojin*	seaweed *algas marinas*	grilled	

Definitions	Vocabulary
1. to do with habits and traditions of a country	**traditional**
2. party when people get married	wedding –
3. something sweet which we eat at the end of a meal	dessert
4. a small portion of food served at the beginning of a meal	appetizer
5. a small pillow ↳ *almohada*	cushion

6. a kind of plant that grows in the ocean or sea	seaweed → algas marinas
7. to rest on the knees	Kneel → arrodillarse niːl pr·
8. not usual, not normal	unusual (anusual) pr
9. an exciting experience or activity	adventure :
10. with a very good, pleasant, special taste → probar -sabor	delicious
11. person who brings the food in a restaurant	server
12. not cooked	raw → crudo
13. great, wonderful, unbelievable → increíble	fantastic
14. with the strong taste of spices	spicy
15. meat or vegetables cooked over low heat for a long time	stew → guiso (estu)pr·
16. a cloth to wash or dry hands	towel → toalla
17. cooked over a fire or on a very hot surface	grilled

B. Choose the correct vocabulary words from the list to fill in the blanks in these sentences. Use each word only once. Not all the words are used in the sentences. Please make changes to verbs or nouns when necessary.

1. The server brought some __appetizers__ first, before the rest of the meal.

2. In many countries people eat a sweet __dessert__ at the end of the meal.

3. There is too much pepper and chili powder in these beans. They are too __spicy__ for me to eat.

4. I just washed my hands. I need a __towel__ to dry them.

5. In that restaurant the servers wear __traditional__ Japanese clothing.

6. You are an excellent cook. Everything tastes __delicious__. or fantastic

7. My friends are getting married. They are having a small __wedding__ party.

8. That lamb __stew__ is delicious but it takes three hours to cook.

9. Do I need to leave a tip for the __server__?

10. She doesn't like __raw__ vegetables. She likes them cooked. Cout (pro)

11. She likes to sit on the floor on a __cushion__.

12. They enjoy travelling because they have many __adventures__ on their trips.

13. People in Japan use a lot of __seaweed__ in their cooking. (niːd pro)

14. In Japanese restaurants sometimes the servers __kneel__ on the floor to take the orders.

15. Camel stew is a very __unusual__ food in North America.

Listening for the Main Ideas

 **Track 44**

A. Listen to the entire interview once or twice and answer the questions. Circle the correct answer for each question.

1. Where are the speakers?
   a. at a restaurant
   b. in Morocco and Japan
   c. on a radio show
   d. in schools

2. Why are they talking about food?
   a. They are planning what they want to have for dinner.
   b. They are talking about the foods and eating habits in countries they visited.
   c. They are describing their favourite foods.
   d. They are deciding which country has the best food.

B. What are the three main topics the interviewer asks each person about? Put a check mark next to the correct statements.

He asks about:

1. differences in foods in different countries
2. differences in shopping for food
3. differences in drinking
4. differences in eating habits
5. a description of their favourite meals
6. differences in restaurants
7. a description of the people

Listening Comprehension

 Track 45

Listen to the conversations as many times as necessary and answer the questions.

1. Where did Bruce eat his special meal?

   He ate it at a traditional Japanese restaurant in a small town.

2. What are two Japanese foods that Bruce thinks are unusual?

   sushi, seaweed, raw fish, squid

3. What is one difference between eating habits in Japan and eating habits in North America?

   warm towel to clean his hans, sitting on the floor, small private room, shopsticks to eat, kneeled on the floor.

4. What are two foods Bruce ate at his special meal?

   sushi, vegetable soup, grilled fish, sake, dessert

5. What are two differences between what people eat and drink in Morocco and what people eat and drink in North America?

a lot spicy, breakfast with stewed beens, drink green tea, camel stew, pigion, a lot of green tea

6. What is one difference between eating habits in Morocco and eating habits in North America?

using hands or bread to eat, sit on cushions on the floor or a low bench.

7. Where did Tanya have her special meal?

Sushi, seaweed

8. What are two foods that Tanya ate at her favourite meal?

Couscous, lamb stew, salad, (eggplant), green tea, plums and olives.

Personalizing

A. Work with a partner and together decide which meal you like better. Explain the reasons for your choice. Then tell your partner about some unusual foods that you tried.

B. Look at the chart below. Answer the questions about yourself and then ask your partner the same questions.

Questions	Me	My Partner
1. How often do you eat out?	Some times, I like take a breakfast or restaurant for special occasions	rarely, she like dinner home
2. What foods from other countries do you sometimes eat?	italian food, greeck food, I like so much, very spicy, not spicy, peruvian food	canadian food vegetable burger
3. Compare the price of restaurant food here and in your home country.	In Colombia is more cheaper and very delicious	more cheap than canada
4. What differences are there between eating habits here and eating habits in your home country?	3 times a day, handwashing before going to the dinner to room	3 timps food drink hot breakfasts lunch 12m 8 dinner
5. What is the most important meal of the day in your home country? Why?	breakfast and lunch because have to have more energy all day for dinner light food	lunch
6. What is the most popular food in your home country?	bandeja paisa, arepa, empanadas, patacones, rellenas and desserts	chapaty and vegetable cooked
7. Is there a food from your home country that you miss having here?	yes, I miss there	yes, she miss there

Vocabulary and Language Chunks

Write the number of the expression next to the meaning. After you check your answers, choose five expressions and write your own sentences.

Expressions

1. to make someone hungry

   tomar un pedido
2. to take an order

   (cenar) comer
3. to have dinner or a meal

   diferente de
4. different from

5. never mind   *hábitos alimenticios*

6. eating habits

7. to sound fantastic

   fuera de este mundo
8. out of this world

9. instead of *en lugar de*

10. to take a trip

11. to get hungry

12. to have tea

Meanings

_9_ to write down what a customer asks for *escribir lo que pide un cliente*

_5_ it doesn't matter *no importa*

_8_ unbelievably good; so good that it seems to be from another world

_6_ ways of eating

_3_ to eat dinner or a meal

_4_ not the same as

_1_ to make someone feel hungry

_11_ to start to feel hungry

_7_ to seem or sound extremely good, wonderful

_9_ in place of *en lugar de*

_12_ to drink tea

_10_ to go on a trip; to travel

SPEAKING 2

Communication Focus 3: Making Excuses and Giving Explanations

When we can't do something, we usually apologize and give an explanation.

Can = present
Could = past

Grammatical Structures	Examples
I'm sorry, I can't + base form of the verb	I'm sorry I can't **go** to the movies tomorrow because I need to study for a test.
I'm sorry, I couldn't + base form of the verb	I'm sorry, I couldn't **meet** you after school yesterday because I had a doctor's appointment.

👥 **SPEAKING ACTIVITY 13**

Work with a partner. Make excuses and role play the situations on the next page. Take turns making excuses. Try to come up with interesting, unusual excuses.

Example:

Teacher/Student

Teacher: Why didn't you study for the test?

Student: I'm sorry, I couldn't study because I was sick.

Speaking STRATEGY

Role playing and working with classmates will give you practice in making conversation in English and will make your speaking skills better.

1. **Teacher/Student**

   Teacher: Why didn't you do your homework?
   come to class last Friday
   hand in your homework
   do your assignment
   see the counsellor
   buy your books
   bring your books to class

2. **Roommates**

   Roommate #1: Why didn't you clean up the kitchen?
   wash the dishes
   vacuum the rug
   take out the garbage
   make your bed
   pay the rent

3. **Friends**

   Friend #1: Why didn't you call me on the weekend?
   come over on Saturday afternoon
   send me an email
   come to the movie on Friday night
   invite me to your party
   come to my birthday party

Communication Focus 4: Talking about Actions in Progress at Specific Times in the Past

The past progressive describes an action in progress at a specific time in the past.

Example:

Last night Diane chatted with friends until 7:00, and then she took a bath.

←— 6:30 PM ——————— 7 PM ——————————— 8 PM —→		
X 6:45	X 7:15 _____	
Diane was	Diane was	
chatting online	taking a bath	

At 6:45, Diane was chatting online.   At 7:15 Diane was taking a bath.

We form the past progressive tense by using the past tense of the verb *to be* and then adding *-ing* to the base form of the verb.

Examples:

The tourists <u>were watching</u> the bears at 4:00 PM.

Everyone <u>was taking</u> pictures at 6:30 PM.

<u>Were</u> you <u>sleeping</u> when I telephoned?

Ellen <u>wasn't working</u> yesterday evening.

SPEAKING ACTIVITY 14

A. Make a quick chart with the headings shown below. Walk around the room and speak to as many classmates as possible. Find out what they were doing at these times.

Names	At 9:00 PM last night . . .	At 10 PM last Saturday night . . .	At 4 PM last Sunday afternoon . . .

B. Write about two people that you spoke to.

SPEAKING ACTIVITY 15

A. Work with a partner to read this description of the students' day. What were the students doing at the times listed below?

Yesterday was an extremely busy day for the Basic English class. At 9:30 in the morning they had their weekly grammar test. The test scared them but they did well on it. After the test at 10:30, they took a short 15-minute break. Then from 10:45 to 11:45 they worked in the computer lab. They wrote stories. At 11:45 they all went out together to a Chinese restaurant for lunch. They got back at 12:45. Then they had a listening comprehension test until 1:30 PM. From 1:45 until 3:00 they practised speaking English in the conversation class. After that they worked on special projects in the library until 3:30. When they left the school just before 4:00 PM, they were very tired and very glad that the day was over.

At 9:45 AM _____ *they were having their weekly grammar test.*

At 10:40 AM _____ they were taking a short break

At 11:00 AM _They were working in the computer lab._
At 12:00 PM _They were having lunch at chinesse restaurant._
At 1:00 PM _they were doing a listening comprehension test._
At 2:00 PM _they were practicing speaking English in the conversation class._
At 3:15 PM _They were working on the special projects in the library_
At 4:00 PM _They were going home, very tired._

B. With your partner, choose a day in the past couple of weeks that your class was very busy. List all the things your class did. Then pick three specific times on that day and tell what your class was doing.

LISTENING 2

Before You Listen

👥 **PRE-LISTENING ACTIVITY**

People usually give reasons or explanations when they can't do something. Work with a partner to look at the following list and think of good reasons or excuses for not doing the actions.

1. I couldn't hand in my homework because _____my dog ate it_____.

2. I can't eat that dish because _____.

3. We couldn't get to class on time because _____.

4. I couldn't clean up the kitchen because _____.

5. I couldn't pass the test because _____.

6. We couldn't come to the party because _____.

7. I can't pay for lunch because _____.

8. I couldn't call you last night because _____.

9. We couldn't go jogging because _____.

PRE-LISTENING VOCABULARY

A. You will hear a conversation on the audio CD that includes the following words. Work with a partner or by yourself to find the definition of each of these words:

fitness	noodles	presentation	terrible	upset
appointment	dentist	excuse	exhausted	turn
assignment	fridge			

Definitions	Vocabulary
1. condition of being physically fit and healthy	**fitness**
2. someone's time to do something	*turn*
3. a task or something to do for a class	*assignment* ✓
4. an appliance used to keep food cold; a refrigerator	*fridge*
5. agreement for a meeting for a special reason	*appointment* ✓
6. an activity in which someone shows, explains, or describes something to a group of people	*presentation* ✓
7. extremely bad	*terrible* ✓
8. a special doctor who looks after teeth and gums	*dentist* ✓
9. very tired	*exhausted* ✓
10. an explanation or reason why something didn't go as planned	*excuse*
11. narrow pieces of dough usually made of flour, eggs, and water, which we cook	*noodles* ✓✓
12. unhappy; disappointed with something	*upset*

B. Choose the correct words from the list above to fill in the blanks in these sentences. Use each word only once. Not all the words are used in the sentences. Please make changes to verbs or nouns when necessary.

1. I'm sorry I couldn't do my homework __**assignment**__.

2. They studied for over six hours and they were __*exhausted*__ *very tired*

3. One of my favourite foods is spicy __*noodles*__.

4. I made an __*appointment*__ and went to the __*dentist*__ because I had a __*terrible*__ toothache.

5. Our group gave a great __*presentation*__ to the class about a trip we took. The teacher gave us a very good mark.

6. He didn't want to help us and his __*excuse*__ was that he felt sick.

7. Why didn't you come to the __*fitness*__ class at the gym?

8. Was the teacher __*upset*__ because all the students were talking when he was teaching?

9. Is it Alice's __*turn*__ to wash the dishes and clean up the kitchen?

Listening for the Main Ideas

Track 46   Listen to the conversations and check off all the things you hear people making excuses for.

✓ **1.** not handing in homework *painting a door, dentist appointment, meet friend, walking his dog*

2. not meeting a friend at the movies

3. not going shopping

4. not making dinner *no meat, no seafood*

5. not meeting a friend at fitness class *friends visiting, he was exhausted*

6. not returning a library book

7. not fixing a car

8. not coming to class *the car broke down*

9. not making a phone call *forgot his phone*

10. not helping make a presentation

11. not going out for dinner *got sick, terrible cold*

Listening Comprehension

A. Listen to the conversations as many times as necessary. In each chart, write in what the person didn't do and his or her excuses.

Track 47

B. Afterward, listen again and write in if the other person accepted the excuse.

Conversation A

What didn't Jake do?	Excuse
1. He didn't go out for dinner with his friends	He got sick.
2. He didn't call.	He took medicine and fell asleep.

Excuse accepted?   YES _____   NO __X__

Conversation B

What didn't Leo do?	Excuse
1. He didn't come to class	his car broke down
2. He didn't call because	he forgot his cellphone

Excuse accepted?   YES _____   NO __X__

Conversation C

What didn't Lucy do?	Excuse
She couldn't cook dinner because there were no eggs and enough think of making pasta.	there was no meat or seafood, vegetables and she didn't
2. She don't have any food	She couldn't see medhool

Excuse accepted?   YES _____   NO __X__

Conversation D

What didn't Phil do?	Excuse
no coming to the fitness class	*friends came over, stay up ate playing games, slept in, he was exhausted*

Excuse accepted?   YES __×__   NO _____

Conversation E

What didn't Eric do?	Excuse
didn't made homework assignment.	*I'm sorry, he going to the dentist.* *I couldn't take my dog for walk.*

Excuse accepted?   YES _____   NO __×__

Personalizing

Work in groups of three. Answer these questions and then find out about the others in your group. Report to the class about the most interesting excuse.

Questions	Me	Partner 1 *Elvira*	Partner 2
When did you last make an excuse for not doing something?	*Last Thursday.*	*Last friday*	
What didn't you do?	*I didn't take a class in the morning*	*In her home she didn't cooke*	
What was your reason?	*because I had a several headache*	*she didn't have times.*	
What was the result? Did the person accept your excuse?	*yes, teacher accepted my excuses*	*yes, her friend accepted her excuses.*	

Vocabulary and Language Chunks

Write the number of the expression next to the meaning. After checking your answers, choose five expressions and write your own sentences.

Words and Expressions

1. to go out for dinner

2. make it *→ hazlo, haz que suceda inventalo*

Meanings

__1__ to eat dinner in a restaurant

__6__ to sleep longer than usual

3. to get sick ✓

4. to have a cold

5. to come over *venir*

6. to sleep in

7. to hand in *entregar*

8. to have an appointment

9. to take (the dog) for a walk

10. to break down

11. kind of *un poco*

12. to let someone know

13. to make supper or a meal

___4___ to give (an assignment) to the teacher

___8___ to have a time for a meeting with someone

___9___ to go for a walk (with the dog)

___5___ to visit someone at their place) *en su casa*

___4___ to be sick with an infection in the nose and throat

___3___ to become sick, ill

___2___ to arrive at a place or an event →*llegar a un lugar o un evento*

___13___ to cook supper or a meal

___12___ to inform someone

___10___ to stop working because of an engine problem

___11___ a little bit; slightly → *levemente* *un poco*

PRONUNCIATION

Pronunciation Focus 1: The Pronunciation of Regular Past Tense Endings

We sometimes pronounce the regular past tense ending *-ed* as a separate syllable, but this is not always the case. For example, if you clap or tap the number of syllables in the word *wanted*, you get two syllables. If you do the same for *loved*, or for *talked*, you get one syllable.

PRONUNCIATION ACTIVITY 2

Listen to these verbs. Put a plus sign next to those verbs in which *-ed* is pronounced as a separate syllable.

 Track 48

1. wanted + *ed*
2. loved *d*
3. stayed *d*
4. tried *d*
5. needed *ed*
6. helped +
7. mashed +
8. cooked +

9. shipped +
10. added + *ed*
11. created + *ed*
12. printed + *ed*
13. sorted + *ed*
14. invited + *ed*
15. boiled *d*

16. talked *talked* +
17. decided + *ed*
18. counted + *ed*
19. seated + *ed*
20. listened *d*
21. opened *d*
22. closed *d*

Track 49

👥 PRONUNCIATION ACTIVITY 3

The regular past tense ending *-ed* can be pronounced as / əd / as in *wanted* or / t / as in *helped* or / d / as in *stayed*.

A. Listen to these verbs and write the pronunciation of the past tense ending that you hear. Write either / t /, / d /, or / əd /.

1. shopped	_t_	8. loved	_d_	15. helped	_t_
2. needed	_əd_	9. landed	_ed_	16. prized	_d_
3. tried	_d_	10. offered	_d_	17. believed	_d_
4. researched	_t_	11. liked	_t_	18. cooked	_t_
5. talked	_t_	12. started	_ed_	19. served	_d_
6. used	_d_	13. added	_ed_	20. introduced	_t_
7. showed	_d_	14. travelled	_d_	21. invented	_ed_

B. Work with a partner to check your answers and then practise saying the verbs.

👥 PRONUNCIATION ACTIVITY 4

Track 50

A. Listen to these sentences and write *present* if the verb is in the present tense or *past* if the verb is in the past tense.

1. _____
2. _____
3. _____
4. _____
5. _____
6. _____
7. _____

B. Work with a partner to check your answers.

C. Take turns with your partner to choose one sentence from each of the pairs below and say it. Your partner will say or write "Present" or "Past" when he or she hears the sentence. Check the answer with your partner after each sentence.

1. a. They travelled to Morocco.   __past__

    b. They travel to Mexico.   __present__

2. a. They use special spices to make the food tasty.   _present_

    b. They used special spices to make the food tasty.   _past_

3. a. They cook the stew in a special pot.   _present_

    b. They cooked the stew in a special pot.   _past_

4. a. North Americans like to eat dinner in front of the TV.   _present_

    b. North Americans liked to eat dinner in front of the TV.   _past_

5. a. Why didn't you cook something with vegetables or eggs?   _past_

    b. Why don't you cook something with vegetables or eggs?   _present_

6. a. The food looked so beautiful.   _past_

    b. The food looks so beautiful.   _present_

7. a. They decorated the food with flowers.   _past_

    b. They decorate the food with flowers.   _present_

PRONUNCIATION ACTIVITY 5

A. Listen and repeat these sentences.   🎧 **Track 51**

1. I waited for you until the last minute.

2. I needed your help with the presentation.

3. Some friends invited me to a wedding and the party lasted for several days.

4. Why didn't you make something with pasta or noodles?

5. I couldn't meet you last Sunday because my friend came over.

6. He had a wonderful trip and tasted some fantastic food.

B. Work with a partner. Read the sentences to him or her and listen to your partner read them to you. Circle any errors that you hear your partner make and then talk about them.

PRONUNCIATION ACTIVITY 6

Work with a partner and tell each other five things that you did last weekend. Use the verbs below. Listen to your partner and write the verbs he or she uses. Check that your partner uses the correct pronunciation.

wash	dress	cook	watch	talk	shop
wish	hope	laugh	work	relax	finish
kiss	mix	joke	bake	cook	dance

PRONUNCIATION ACTIVITY 7

A. Listen to the questions and then write them.   🎧 **Track 52**

Questions

1. _Did you have anything to eat?_
2. _Did he buys some chocolate?_
3. _When did you order chinese food?_
4. _Where did you go and what did you do?_
5. _Why did you come to fitness class?_
6. _Did I hurt you?_ → _te bastime_
7. _What did you say?_
8. _How did you do that?_
9. _How often do you eat spicy food?_
10. _What were you doing when I called you?_

B. Work with a partner to check your questions and then make up an answer to each question.

Answers

1. _yes I do_ _____
2. _____
3. _____
4. _____
5. _____

6. _____
7. _____
8. _____
9. _____
10. _____

Pronunciation Focus 2: Consonant Clusters

A consonant cluster is two or more consonant sounds pronounced together. In English, we can have two or three consonants coming together at the beginnings or ends of words.

Words Beginning or Ending with Two Consonants	Words Beginning or Ending with Three Consonants
dress	**str**eet
drink	**str**ing
cream	**spr**ing
dres**sed**	mi**xed**
lau**ghed**	co**lds**
answe**red**	pa**rks**

 **PRONUNCIATION ACTIVITY 8**

Track 53

A. Listen to the words. For each pair, put a check mark next to the word you hear.

1. bread ✓   bed
2. foot   fruit ✓
3. snack   sack
4. skid   squid
5. Sue   stew
6. clean   keen
7. dry   die
8. bother   brother
9. bake   break

10. played   paid
11. pretty   pity
12. back   black
13. carts   cart
14. script   scripts
15. ask   asked
16. jumped   jump
17. fix   fixed

B. Check your answers with the class.

C. Work with a partner. For each pair, say one of the words to your partner. Your partner must point to (or spell) the word he or she heard. Give feedback after each.

PRONUNCIATION ACTIVITY 9

Track 54

A. Listen to the words. For each pair, put a check mark next to the word you hear.

1. shopped ✓	shop	9. nights	nice
2. wash ✓	washed	10. once	one
3. feel	field ✓	11. went	when
4. kneeled	kneel	12. spelled	spell
5. cold	coal	13. beards	beers
6. answer	answered	14. script	scripts
7. built	bill	15. Xerox	Xeroxed
8. schedule	scheduled		

B. Check your answers with the class.

C. Work with a partner. For each pair, say one word to your partner. Your partner must point to (or spell) the word he or she heard. Give feedback after each.

PRONUNCIATION ACTIVITY 10

Track 55

A. Listen to the words. Repeat each word.

B. Listen again and write each word you hear. There will be 30 words altogether.

_____ _____ _____ _____ _____

_____ _____ _____ _____ _____

_____ _____ _____ _____ _____

_____ _____ _____ _____ _____

_____ _____ _____ _____ _____

_____ _____ _____ _____ _____

C. Check your work with the class and then work with a partner to put the words into the correct categories on the next page.

People	Things to Eat or Drink	Things to Wear	How People Feel

COMMUNICATING IN THE REAL WORLD

A. Use your English to talk to people outside your classroom. On your own or with a partner, talk to five people outside your class. Ask them the questions below and record the information. Make a short report to the class about what you learned.

Before you begin, say this:

> May I ask you some questions? This is an assignment for my English class.

1. a. What is your favourite food?
    b. What is your favourite drink?
    c. What is your favourite snack?

2. How often do you eat out? What's your favourite restaurant?

3. How often do you eat take-out food? What's your favourite take-out food?

4. When did you last make an excuse for not doing something?

5. What excuse did you make? What happened?

B. Choose one:

1. Go to one of the many websites that are all about food. Your teacher will have some suggestions. Write down some new words about food and food preparation that you learn there. Teach these words to your classmates.

    OR

2. Find a recipe that you like and explain it to your class.

    OR

3. Project:
    a. Alone or with a partner, take pictures of different kinds of food—these can be in restaurants or they can be dishes that you or a friend cooked.
    b. Make a presentation to the class about four of your pictures. Talk about the kind of food or dish this is and why you chose it. What country is it from? When do people eat it? What do they eat it with? What is in the dish? How do you prepare and cook the dish? Be prepared to answer questions.

SELF-EVALUATION

Think about your work in this chapter. For each row in the chart sections Grammar and Language Functions, Learning Strategies, and Pronunciation, give yourself a score based on the rating scale below and write a comment in the Notes section.

Show the chart to your teacher. Talk about what you need to do to make your English better.

Rating Scale

| 1 | 2 | 3 | 4 | 5 |

Needs improvement. ← ————————————————→ *Great!*

	Score	Notes
Grammar and Language Functions		
talking about food and eating habits		
using countable and uncountable nouns		
narrating stories and events which happened in the past		
using the regular past tense, including questions and negatives, and time expressions		
using the irregular past tense including questions, negatives, and time expressions		
asking questions and making statements about actions in progress in the past		
making a short presentation		
making excuses and give explanations		
Pronunciation		
recognizing and pronouncing regular past tense endings		
recognizing and pronouncing consonant clusters at the beginning and end of words		
Learning Strategies		
Speaking		
role playing and working with classmates to get practice in making conversation in English and improve my speaking skills		

paying attention to verb forms and using the correct tense so that other people understand when events happened		

Listening

listening for time expressions to understand the order of events		

Vocabulary and Language Chunks

Look at this list of new vocabulary and language chunks you learned in this chapter. Give yourself a score based on the rating scale and write a comment.

to make someone hungry	out of this world	to get sick
to take an order	instead of	to have a cold
to have dinner	to take a trip	to come over
different from	to get hungry	to sleep in
never mind	to have tea	to hand in
eating habits	to go out for dinner	to have an appointment
to sound fantastic	to make it	to take (the dog) for a walk
kind of	to let someone know	to break down
to make supper or a meal		

	Score	Notes
understanding new vocabulary and language chunks		
using new words and phrases correctly		

Write six sentences and use new vocabulary you learned in this chapter.

1. _____
2. _____
3. _____
4. _____
5. _____
6. _____

My plan for practising is _____

_____

_____

_____

CHAPTER 6

Let the Good Times Roll

Holidays and Special Celebrations

Expressing future plans and intentions

Talking about seasons and the weather

Making predictions

Stating intentions

Inviting people to do activities

THINKING AND TALKING

A. Work with a partner. What are the people in the pictures celebrating? Choose one picture and tell a story about it. Answer some of these questions in your story:

> Who are these people?
>
> Where are they?
>
> What are they doing?
>
> How do they feel?
>
> What do you think happened before?
>
> What are they planning to do next?

Find another pair of students and tell your stories to each other. Report about the story you like the best.

B. Work in groups. Match the holidays with the months or dates. Then talk about how people celebrate these holidays. Make sentences using the celebration activities listed below.

New Year's Day	December 25
Valentine's Day	November 11
St Patrick's Day	January 1
Thanksgiving Day	Third Monday in May
Christmas	July 1
Boxing Day	February 14
Victoria Day	March 17
Remembrance Day	Third Monday in October
New Year's Eve	First Monday in September
Labour Day	December 26
Canada Day	December 31

Celebration Activities

wear something green and have parades

return Christmas gifts and shop at sales

wear poppies and remember the war dead

give chocolates and flowers to their sweethearts

decorate Christmas trees and give each other gifts

have parties and sing "Auld Lang Syne"

have parades and parties for workers

usually start planting their gardens

have picnics and sing "O Canada"

eat turkey and pumpkin pie

Example:

> Christmas is on December 25. People decorate Christmas trees and give each other gifts at this time.

SPEAKING ACTIVITY 1

Work in groups of four. Discuss these questions and report to the class.

1. What is the most recent holiday that you celebrated?

2. How did you celebrate?

3. What is the most important holiday in your home country?

4. How do people celebrate the holiday? What special things do they do?

5. What is the special food on this holiday? Where do people eat it?

6. What is your favourite holiday? Explain why you like it.

7. Some people say that we don't have enough holidays. Do you agree? Do you think we should have more holidays? When should we have these new holidays and what should we do to celebrate?

SPEAKING 1

Communication Focus 1: Expressing Future Plans and Intentions

We can use *to be going to* + the base form of the verb to talk about future plans and intentions.

Grammar Note: Using *to be going to*

These are the grammar structures we use to express future plans and intentions.

Affirmative	Contractions
I am going to celebrate Valentine's Day.	I'm going to celebrate Valentine's Day.
He is going to buy a present.	He's going to buy a present.
She is going to bake a cake.	She's going to bake a cake.
It is going to be fun.	It's going to be fun.
We are going to have a party.	We're going to have a party.
You are going to get a birthday card.	You're going to get a birthday card.
They are going to enjoy themselves.	They're going to enjoy themselves.

Questions	Negatives
Am I going to celebrate Valentine's Day?	I'm not going to celebrate Valentine's Day.
Is he going to buy a present?	He isn't going to buy a present.
Is she going to bake a cake?	She isn't going to bake a cake.
Is it going to be fun?	It isn't going to be fun.
Are we going to have a party?	We aren't going to have a party.
Are you going to get a birthday card?	You aren't going to get a birthday card.
Are they going to enjoy themselves?	They aren't going to enjoy themselves.

We can use *to be going to* + base form of verb with the following time expressions.

tomorrow	next year	in a few weeks
tomorrow night	next week	in an hour
	next _____	in _____

 SPEAKING ACTIVITY 2

 Track 56

Make a quick chart with the headings shown below. Walk around the room and talk to as many people as possible. Ask them what they are going to do on these holidays. What are you going to do . . .

Names	Next New Year's Eve	Next Valentine's Day	Next Christmas

👤 PRONUNCIATION ACTIVITY 1: *TO BE GOING TO* AND *GONNA*

When people speak quickly in North America, they often pronounce *going to* as *gonna*. We don't use *gonna* in writing, but people often use this in speaking.

Listen and write out the complete sentence. Don't use *gonna* in your sentence.

1. _____.   6. _____.
2. _____.   7. _____.
3. _____.   8. _____.
4. _____.   9. _____.
5. _____.   10. _____.

👥 SPEAKING ACTIVITY 3

First, make questions using the words in the first column. Then, work in groups of three and ask your partners the questions. Report about two interesting plans.

Questions	Partner 1	Partner 2
What / do after school? **Example: What are you going to do after school?**		
What time / get home tonight?		
What time / eat supper?		
What / do after supper?		
What time / go to bed?		
What time / get up tomorrow?		
Where / be on the weekend?		
What / do on the weekend?		
What / do after you finish this English program?		

👥 SPEAKING ACTIVITY 4

Work in groups of four to plan a party for the last day of your class. Make decisions about all the topics below. Then, when you are finished, make a presentation to the class about your plan for the class party. Use a poster or another visual aid such as PowerPoint in your presentation. The class will vote for the best party.

Location: Where are you going to have the party?
                   What kind of decorations are you going to have?
                   Who is going to be responsible for the decorations?

Time: When are you going to have the party?
                     What time is the party going to begin and end?

Refreshments: What kind of food are you going to have?
                     How much food are you going to have?
                     Where are you going to get the food?
                     What kind of drinks are you going to have?

Entertainment: What kind of music are you going to have?
                     Where are you going to get the music?
                     Who is going to be the DJ?

Other Ideas:

_____

_____

_____

Communication Focus 2:
Talking about Seasons and the Weather

In North America, these are the four seasons and the months of the year.

Winter	Spring	Summer	Autumn/Fall
December 21	March 21	June 21	September 21
January	April	July	October
February	May	August	November
March	June	September	December

Work with a partner. In the chart below, describe the weather in each month. Use the sentences listed. Write down all the weather possibilities. Compare your answers. Choose a month and tell the class what the weather is usually like in that month.

Some Ways to Describe the Weather

It snows.	It's sunny.	It is windy.
It rains.	It's raining.	There are snow flurries.
It is cold.	It's humid.	It is foggy. *esta nublado*
It is hot.	It's overcast. *esta nublado*	There are blizzards. *there aren't*
It is warm.	*las rutas congeladas* The roads are icy.	It is cloudy.
It is cool.	There are thunderstorms.	There is freezing rain and sleet.
It is mild.	There are showers.	The snow and ice melts.

January	February	March	April	May	June
It snows. It is cold. There are snow flurries. There are blizzards. The roads are icy.	It cold it snow flurries There are blizzard the roads are icy.	it snows it is cold there are snow flurries There are blizzard The road are icy	it is windy it's raining there is freezing rain and sleet	There are thunderstorms. it's raining The snow and ice melts it is mild it is sunny	it is cool it is mild There are Thunderstorms it is sunny it's raining There are showers

July	August	September	October	November	December
there are showers it is hot it is warm it is sunny it's humid	it is warm There are showers it is warm there are showers	it is windy there are thunderstorms it is cool it rains	it is cloudy it is fuggy it is windy it sunny it snows	it is overcast it is windy it is cloudy it is cold there are flurries	it is cold it is snow it is windy There are blizzard

ÅÅ SPEAKING ACTIVITY 5

A. Work with a partner. Go to a weather website. Your teacher will give you some websites to choose from. Find out what the weather is going to be like in your city on the following days. What do you and your partner think about the weather forecasts? Report to the class.

Date	Weather Forecast
Tomorrow	the weather going to be 18?
Two weeks from today	the weather going to be low temperature and raining.
Four weeks from today	4 semanas a partir de hoy the weather going to be cold and rainy

B. Go to one of the websites again to find the answer to this question: What's the weather going to be like tomorrow in these world cities?

Beijing   New York   Chicago

Seoul   Vancouver   Tokyo

What's the weather going to be like in two other cities you are interested in?

1. _____

2. _____

👥 SPEAKING ACTIVITY 6

Work with a partner. Ask each other these questions and report to the class.

1. What month and season is your birthday in?
2. What is the weather usually like on your birthday?
3. What do you usually do on your birthday?
4. What kind of weather would you like to have on your birthday? Explain.
5. What do people usually do to celebrate birthdays in your home country?
6. What are you going to do on your next birthday?

👥 SPEAKING ACTIVITY 7

Work with a partner. Go to a website about birthday traditions (your teacher will give you the URL) and find out the answers to these questions. Then find out and report about birthday traditions in another country you are interested in.

1. How did the birthday song start?
2. How did birthday parties start?
3. What is the history of the birthday cake?
4. What is the history of birthday candles?

👥 SPEAKING ACTIVITY 8

Work with a partner. Ask each other these questions. Report to the class about your similarities and differences.

Questions	Me	My Partner
1. You are going to celebrate your friend's birthday. What gift are you going to give?		
2. You are going to go to a friend's house for dinner. What gift are you going to bring?		
3. It's Christmas. What are you going to give your best friend?		

continued on next page

Questions	Me	My Partner
4. It's Valentine's Day. What are you going to give your sweetheart?		
5. It's Mother's Day. What are you going to give your mother?		
6. You are going to go to a friend's wedding. What gift are you going to give?		
7. You are going to visit a friend in the hospital. What gift are you going to take?		
8. Your friend just bought a new house. What gift are you going to give?		
9. On what other occasions do you give gifts? What do you usually give?		

👫 SPEAKING ACTIVITY 9

Often we make statements about the weather to start a conversation. Work with a partner and put a check mark next to those statements on the list that we can use to start a conversation. Then find an answer to the statement on the list. Choose five conversation openers and responses and practise saying them.

Example:

> What wonderful weather we're having!
>
> Yes, I just love it!

What wonderful weather we are having! ✓

Hot enough for you? *lo suficiente mente caliente para ti.*

What terrible weather! → *que clima horrible!*

Yes, it sure is. → *si seguro que lo es.*

Beautiful day, isn't it? → *hermoso día, no?*

You can say that again! → *puedes decir eso otra vez !*

How about this weather! *Que tal este clima?*

I can't believe it. → *no puedo creerlo*

I heard it's going to be a rainy weekend. → *escuche que va a ser un fin de semana lluvioso.*

Yes, it's raining cats and dogs!

Don't you just love this spring weather?

I know. It's incredible.

Yes, I just love it.

I know. I can't stand it.

That's too bad.

It's my favourite.

LISTENING 1

Before You Listen

👥 PRE-LISTENING ACTIVITY

A. Work with a partner to answer these questions.

What holidays are people celebrating in these pictures?

Where do you think they are?

What other things are they going to do to celebrate?

lunar New year

B. Work with a partner. Find out the following information from your partner and report to the class.

Questions	My Partner's Answers
What country are you from?	libane
When do people celebrate the New Year in your home country? how many days.	January 1º
How long does the New Year's celebration last?	start DIC 31 night finis Ja-
What special things do people do to celebrate?	new clothes, family party
What special foods do they eat?	meet, Kestane
What do people do for good luck?	broken the glaces is good luck
What kind of resolutions do people make?	reflexion about the bad think for changes the new year

C. These are some unusual customs to celebrate the arrival of the New Year in different countries. Work with a partner to match the custom to the country. Guess if you do not know the answer.

Countries

~~Colombia~~   South Africa   ~~Ireland~~   Mexico   Russia   ~~Romania~~

1. Trying to hear farm animals speaking <u>is a New Year's Eve custom in Romania</u>.

2. Hitting the walls with bread to scare off bad spirits
   <u>Ireland</u>.

3. Throwing old appliances and furniture out of windows
tirar los viejos electrodomesticos por la ventana
_____South Africa (Italy)_____.

4. Wearing red underwear for good luck __(China), Mexico__.
ropa interior

5. Walking around the block with empty suitcases to have a year
filled with travel _____Colombia_____.

6. Writing a wish on a piece of paper, burning the paper, putting
un deseo
the ash into a glass of champagne, and drinking it by 12:01 AM
_____Russia_____.

PRE-LISTENING VOCABULARY

A. You will hear a conversation on the audio CD that includes the
following words. Work with a partner or by yourself to find the
definition of each word.

festival	resolution	dragon	pot *macetu*	harvest *cosecho*
worries	scarecrow *espanta parjaros*	shiny *brillante*	gift
arrival	raisins *pasas*	huge *enorme* *use*	to wrap *envolver*

Definitions	Vocabulary
1. a time when there are special events and people celebrate	**festival**
2. a very large lizard-like monster which does not really exist	dragon
3. dried grapes	raisins
4. a strong decision to do or not to do something, usually made on New Year's Eve	resolution
5. bright and glossy; reflecting light	shiny
6. something made to look like a person to scare birds away	scarecrow
7. a container made of glass or metal for cooking; a container for plants	pot
8. problems, concerns	worries
9. very big	huge iuge
10. a present; something we give to someone	gift
11. the act of arriving	arrival
12. to cover; to put paper or other material around something	to wrap
13. time when people gather or pick the things they grow	harvest

B. Choose the correct words from the list to fill in the blanks in these
sentences. Use each word only once. Not all the words are used
in the sentences. Please make changes to verbs or nouns when
necessary.

1. People everywhere enjoy celebrating holidays and __festivals__.

2. She has a lot of __worries__. She has problems with her health
and her job.

3. In China, children get a ___gift___ of money at New Year's celebrations.

4. In Iran, people plant seeds in small ___pots___ at New Year's.

5. In some places the ___arrival___ of spring is the start of the new year.

6. At ___harvest___ time people pick all the fruit and vegetables that they grow.

7. She made a New Year's ___resolution___ to quit smoking.

8. Chinese New Year's celebrations always include a ___dragon___ dance.

9. A dragon isn't a small animal. It's ___huge (huch) pr.___

10. The Portuguese eat ___raisins___ at midnight on New Year's Eve.

11. She likes silver because it's ___shiny___.

12. Let's ___wrap___ the present in bright paper to surprise her.
   ___(rap)pr___

Listening for the Main Ideas

 **Track 57**   Listen to the report and answer the questions.

1. What is this report about? Check each one that applies.

   ___✓___ New Year's celebrations in different cultures

   ___✓___ the different dates for the new year

   ___✗___ the different kinds of food people eat at New Year's celebrations.

   ___✗___ the different kinds of things people say at New Year's celebrations.

2. What are some things that are different in New Year's celebrations?

   ___✓___ the time of the new year

   ___✓___ the way in which people celebrate the new year

   ___✗___ how long they celebrate

3. What are some things that are the same in New Year's celebrations?

   ___✗/✓___ the songs and the music are the same   _Auld lang syne – days gone by_

   ___✓___ everyone celebrates the beginning of a new year

   ___✓___ everyone hopes for a better future

   ___✗___ the food is the same

Listening Comprehension

Track 58   Listen to the report as many times as necessary and answer the questions.

A. When is the New Year celebration in these countries?

1. Spain _____December 31 and January 1_____

2. USA _____Dic 31 – Jan 1_____

3. Iran _____first day of Spring March 20th last 2 weeks_____

4. China _____lete January or, Febrory_____

5. Ecuador _____December 31st goodbye old year vello New year_____

B. In what countries do people do these things?

1. Sing "Auld Lang Syne"   CANADA,   **USA** , EUROPE.

2. Burn a scarecrow   _____Ecuator_____

3. Give money wrapped in red paper   _____CHina_____

4. Throw pots of plants into rivers   _____Ira...._____

5. Eat 12 raisins at midnight   _____Portugal_____

6. Watch fireworks   _____chine._____

7. Wear new clothes   _____chino_____

8. Watch a huge shiny ball come down   _____New York city_____

Listening STRATEGY

Check to see how much you understand. Try to find out why you don't understand sometimes. This will help make your listening comprehension better.

go to restarrent

visite f. onif.

Personalizing

Work in groups of four. Find out the answers to these questions and report to the class.

	Where were you last New Year's Eve and what did you do to celebrate?	What New Year's resolutions did you make?	Where are you going to be and what are you going to do next New Year's Eve?	What New Year's resolutions are you going to make?	Where would you like to be and how would you like to spend the perfect New Year's Eve?
Me	Colombia	Colombia with friends Ofamily			
Partner 1	Adhanon Calgary	in Calgary his famil			
Partner 2	Da noose party family in Edmonton	In family at home dront much			
Partner 3	Kashimir in Calgary Covid				

Vocabulary and Language Chunks

Write the number of the expression next to the meaning. After checking your answers choose five expressions and write your own sentences.

Words and Expressions	Meanings
1. all over	__1__ in all places
2. around the world	__12__ to firmly decide to do something
3. to have parties	__7__ for good fortune
4. to crowd into	__11__ to represent, symbolize
5. to dress up	__10__ to throw away; to be free of, to not have anymore
6. to make a wish	__9__ to eat a meal outside in the open air, for fun
7. for good luck	__5__ to put special clothes on
8. to clean up	__6__ to wish for
9. to go on a picnic	__2__ everywhere in the world
10. to get rid of	__3__ to organize and plan parties
11. to stand for	__4__ to move large numbers of people or things into a smaller space
12. to make a resolution	__8__ to make clean and tidy

Communication Focus 3: Making Predictions

We can use *will* + the base form of the verb, or *to be going to* + the base form of the verb, to make predictions about the future. We also use *will* + the base form of the verb to express promises and offers.

Examples:

In 2050, people won't drive cars.

It's going to snow tomorrow.

I am going to become rich and famous.

I'll call you later.

Grammar Note: Using *will*

These are the forms of *will* + the base form of the verb.

Affirmative	Question Forms	Negative
I will work. / I'll work.	Will I work?	I won't work.
He will study. / He'll study.	Will he study?	He won't study.
She will come. / She'll come.	Will she come?	She won't come.
It will snow. / It'll snow.	Will it snow?	It won't snow.
We will understand. / We'll understand.	Will we understand?	We won't understand.
They will try. / They'll try.	Will they try?	They won't try.

SPEAKING ACTIVITY 10

A. At the beginning of a new year, the media often ask famous fortune tellers or seers to make predictions about the coming year. Imagine that you are a seer. Make predictions about what will happen in 10 years about the following topics.

Example:

> In 10 years I will speak English perfectly, and I will be an English teacher.

Topics	Predictions
you	In Two years I will speak English perfectly. and I will open my beauty salon.
your teacher	After speak English perfectly I will be a teacher.
your city	I will visite my city next January
your school	In 2024 I will study business.
fashions	next year I will change my clothes because I am going to be rich and famous
medicine	Science will find/develop/make a cure for Cancer.
a famous celebrity	I one year I will bring my grandson Thiago and his mom to live here.
sports	In 2024 I will practice Yoga.

B. Work in groups of four. Tell each other your predictions. Which predictions were the same? What were the most interesting predictions?

SPEAKING ACTIVITY 11

Work in groups. Choose five topics from the list below and make predictions about what you think will happen by the year 2050. Give reasons for your predictions. Report your group's predictions to the class.

Example:

personal computers	People won't use personal computers because everyone will use their phones and watches to surf the Internet.

weather	the English language	women
tourism and travel	Mandarin (Chinese language)	cars
men	population of the world	music

Our group's predictions:

1. _____

2. _____

3. _____

4. _____

5. _____

SPEAKING ACTIVITY 12

Below are some common superstitions in North America. Work with a partner. Talk to some native speakers of English outside the class and ask them about these superstitions. Then write what each one means and report to the class.

Example:

If you break a mirror . . .

What will happen if you break a mirror?

If you break a mirror you will have seven years of bad luck.

If you walk under a ladder . . .

_bad luck_____

_____

If you open an umbrella in the house . . .

_they will bring bad luck_____

_____

If you find a four-leaf clover . . .

_It is a good luck_____

_____

If a black cat crosses your path . . .

it is a bad luck → something bad might happen.

_____

If you cross your fingers . . .

you might stop something or something bad from happening

_____

If you put shoes on the table . . .

you will have bad luck for the rest of the day.

_____

If your ears ring or burn . . .

It's because someone is talking bad about you.

LISTENING 2

Before You Listen

PRE-LISTENING ACTIVITY

A. Work with a partner to read the paragraph below and put a check mark next to all the possible gifts on the list that you think Plan Canada gives to people in developing countries.

A Different Kind of Gift

Plan Canada is an organization that gives gifts to people in poor countries because it wants these people to have a better life. Plan Canada started in 1937 and is one of the oldest and largest organizations in the world doing this kind of work. It does not work for profit and it has only one goal—to improve the lives of children. Plan Canada works in 69 countries around the world including Africa, Asia, and the Americas. It gives children and their families the things they need to improve their lives.

Possible Gifts

baby chicks baby chiken	seeds, tools, and training to grow food ✓	clean water for families ✓
money gift cards	checkups for newborn babies ✓	goats
jewellery ✗	books ✓	two pigs ✗
toys	clothes ✗	ten fruit trees
school supplies for one child ✓	sheep ✗	shampoo and soap ✓

Go to Plan Canada's website to check if your answers are correct.

Then find out about four other gifts they give and list them here. Report to the class.

1. _____ help to refugees, farmar/teacher
2. _____ pharmacy supplies
3. _____ mosquito nets
4. _____ school meals

B. With your partner, talk about three gifts that would make life easier for a poor family in this city. Explain your ideas. Report to the class.

PRE-LISTENING VOCABULARY

A. You will hear a conversation on the audio CD that includes the following words. Work with a partner or by yourself to find the definition of each word. Please make changes to the verbs or nouns if necessary.

to earn   donations   belongings   infected
to head   impoverished   HIV/AIDS   appreciative
distributor   flooring   bucks   to appreciate
mission   goat   apiece   herd

Definitions	Vocabulary
1. a very serious illness which originated in Africa and has spread all over the world	HIV/AIDS
2. a special job; task	mission
3. things that belong to someone	belongings / posesions
4. things such as money, food, or clothes that people give to help an organization	donations
5. being sick or having the germs of a disease in one's body	infected
6. to go towards; to move in the direction of	to head to
7. materials which we put on a floor	flooring
8. another word for *dollars*	bucks
9. very poor	impoverished
10. a small domesticated animal with horns that people keep for milk and meat	goat
11. to understand or recognize the value of something /someone	to appreciate
12. feeling and showing gratefulness and appreciation	appreciative
13. someone who buys and resells products to others	distributor
14. a group of animals such as cows	herd
15. to get something, such as money, in return for work	to earn
16. each	apiece

B. Choose the correct words from the list to fill in the blanks in these sentences. Not all the words are used in the sentences. Use each word only once. Please make changes to the nouns or verbs if necessary.

1. ___HIV/AIDS___ is a terrible disease which kills many people.

2. She tries to help _impoverished_ women in Africa make a living.

3. Those chickens cost 25 ___bucks___ ___apiece___.

4. Her friends make ___donations___ to help the poor women in Kenya.

5. If they look after the animals, the women ___earn___ enough money to buy food for their families.

6. When you get off the plane, please take all your _belongings_ with you.

7. The women were happy to get the gifts. They were very _appreciative_.

8. She is going to go to Kenya on a charity _mission_ to help women.

9. He is a _distributor_, which means that he sells things to other stores.

10. They want to change the floors in their new house. They are going to shop for _flooring_.

11. Thanks for your help. I really _appreciate_ it.

12. We call a group of ducks a flock of ducks but a group of goats is a _herd_ of goats.

13. When the class was over, everyone _headed_ towards the doors to leave.

Listening for the Main Ideas

Listen to the news report and put a check mark next to all the correct statements.

🎧 **Track 59**

1. Why is this story in the news?
   Marie McKay raises money to help people in Africa. ✓
   She is going to give goats away for free. ✓
   Marie McKay is going to bring African women to Vancouver. ✗
   Marie McKay raises money from her friends and family. ✓

2. What do the reporters think about the woman?
   They think she is selfish. ✗
   They think she is generous. ✓
   She cares about Kenyan women and their country. ✓
   They are surprised at her story. ✓
   They think she is a good businesswoman. ✗

Listening Comprehension

Listen to the news report as many times as necessary. Write *T* if the statement is true and *F* if it is false.

🎧 **Track 60**

1. Marie McKay is going to Kenya. — T
2. She works for a charity organization. — F
3. She collects things to give to people in Kenya. — F
4. She is taking a lot of her personal belongings with her. — F
5. She will give goats to all the poor women in Kenya. — F
6. She will buy the goats in Canada. — F

7. The women will sell the milk from the goats.   _T_

8. Marie McKay gets the money to buy the goats from friends.   _T_

9. One friend is giving her enough money for 100 goats.   _T_

10. The cost of a goat is $14 each.   _F_

11. The year before this report she gave away 300 goats.   _T_

12. Marie McKay loves helping people in Kenya.   _T_

13. She spends six weeks a year in Kenya.   _F_

Personalizing

A. Work in groups of four. Do you agree with these statements? Why or why not? Discuss.

1. It's a good idea for rich countries to help poorer countries.

2. It's a good idea for rich people to give at least 10 percent of their income to help poor people.

3. The best way to help poor people and countries is to give them money.

4. People in poor countries appreciate gifts from abroad.

B. What charities do you think people in this city should give money to?

Vocabulary and Language Chunks

Write the number of the expression next to the meaning. After checking your answers choose five expressions and write your own sentences.

Words and Expressions	Meanings
1. to save up	_12_ a little
2. to head straight to	_8_ a group of animals
3. word gets around	_7_ having a special job or task to do
4. to give away	_10_ to get and eat food
5. to pay one's own way	_6_ to prepare
6. to get ready	_5_ to pay for oneself
7. on a mission	_3_ information spreads; people talk about news
8. a herd of	_2_ to go directly to
9. to take along	_1_ to put away, to keep, to save
10. to feed oneself	_4_ to give to someone without payment
12. a bit	_9_ to take with you
13. plenty of	_14_ a very strong feeling of love for
14. a love affair	_13_ a lot of/a great deal of

SPEAKING 2

Communication Focus 4: Stating Plans, Arrangements, and Intentions

We can use the present progressive tense *to be* + base + *-ing* to state plans, arrangements, or intentions. We also need to use a future time adverbial such as *tomorrow*, *after school*, *next week*.

Examples:

> We're having a test next week.
>
> Are you going out for coffee after school?
>
> I'm not leaving until 5 PM.

SPEAKING ACTIVITY 13

Make a quick chart with the headings shown below. Walk around the room and find out the answers to these questions from your classmates.

What are you doing after class tomorrow?

What are you doing on Saturday night?

When are you getting together with friends?

Names	After class tomorrow?	On Saturday night?	Getting together with friends?

Communication Focus 5: Inviting People to Do Activities

When we invite people to do things we can use one of these expressions.

Expressions	Invitations	Answers
Would you like to + base form of the verb	**Would you like to** go out for coffee after school?	Yes. I'd love to. Yes, I'd like that.
How about + verb + *-ing*	**How about** going out for coffee after school?	I'm sorry, I can't. I have to meet my mother then.
Do you want to + base form of verb *Do you feel like* + verb + *-ing*	**Do you want to** go out for coffee after school? **Do you feel like** going out for coffee after school?	Sure. That will be fun. That sounds great. That's a great idea.

SPEAKING ACTIVITY 14

Work with a partner. Practise the example conversation and then make up five conversations to practise inviting. Invite your partner to some of these places.

1. dinner at your place
2. the movies
3. a birthday party
4. a potluck dinner at your place
5. a New Year's Eve party
6. a house-warming party
7. a picnic
8. a concert

Example:

Partner A: What are you doing after school on Friday?

Partner B: I'm going to the library to study.

Partner A: Would you like to go out for something to eat after that?

Partner B: Sure. That's a great idea.

SPEAKING ACTIVITY 15

On the calendar below, fill in the activities you plan to or need to do in the next week. Write in your English classes, appointments, clubs, and gym classes.

Then walk around the room and make dates with people to do one of the following activities.

go out for dinner   go shopping   go bowling   play cards

go for a walk   go jogging   go swimming   play tennis

play Ping-Pong   go skating   play badminton   go fishing

	Monday	Tuesday	Wednesday	Thursday	Friday	Saturday	Sunday
Morning				go ·			
Afternoon							
Evening							

When you find someone who is free and accepts your invitation, write his or her name and the activity in the correct box and also write the name and activity of invitations you accept. Continue inviting people until you have five dates with five people. Don't forget you can only make and accept dates for times when you are free.

PRONUNCIATION

Pronunciation Focus 1: The /a/ Sound as in *got* and the /ow/ Sound as in *goat*

 **Track 61**

PRONUNCIATION ACTIVITY 2

Listen to these words with the vowel sound /a/. Repeat the words.

1. hot	**4.** not	**7.** got
2. stop	**5.** job	**8.** cost
3. pot	**6.** bought	**9.** caught

 **Track 62**

PRONUNCIATION ACTIVITY 3

Listen to these words with the vowel sound /ow/. Repeat the words.

1. goat	**4.** coat	**7.** boat	**10.** home
2. note	**5.** tote	**8.** alone	
3. Joan	**6.** float	**9.** rode	

 **Track 63**

PRONUNCIATION ACTIVITY 4

A. Listen to these pairs of words. Circle *same* if the vowel sounds in both words are the same. Circle *different* if the vowel sounds are different.
Examples:

bought	boat	(different)
hot	hot	(same)

1. same	(different)		7. same	(different)
2. same	(different)		8. same	(different)
3. same	(different)		9. same	(different)
4. (same)	different		10. same	(different)
5. same	(different)		11. same	(different)
6. (same)	different			

B. Check your work and then work with a partner to make up four sentences with some of these words. Practise saying the sentences to your partner.

 **Track 64**

PRONUNCIATION ACTIVITY 5

A. Listen to these sentences. Fill in the blanks with the missing words.

1. She ___got___ 300 ___goats___ to give away to ___poor___ women.

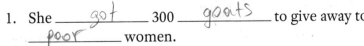

2. They ___brought___ ___pots___ for the ___hot___ food.

3. This ___coat___ ___cost___ the most in that shop.

4. She ___bought___ that ___robe___ → *tunica*

5. ___Joan___ fell in love with ___John___.

6. She ___thought___ them to ___talk___ clearly.

7. They ___bought___ their ___own___ ___boats___.

B. Work with a partner to practise saying the sentences.

👥 PRONUNCIATION ACTIVITY 6

A. Work with a partner and choose five words that you use often that have the sound / a / or the sound / ow /. Make sentences with these words.

1. I bought the pots for my home.
2. I bought a boars for this winter.
3. I brought a new coat to my mom.   *broat (pron)*   *broat*   *cout*
4. I like your new boats.
5. I stay alone in my home.
   This scrives a hot pots for the costumers.

B. Practise saying the sentences with your partner.

Pronunciation Focus 2: Falling Intonation

Track 65

When we end a *wh-* question, a statement, or a command, the voice falls to its lowest pitch level.   *Monotone for intonation or natural intonation*

Listen to these sentences.
Examples:

It's snowing in Toronto. ↘

How old are you? ↘

When is Boxing Day? ↘

Don't worry. ↘

🧍 PRONUNCIATION ACTIVITY 7

Track 66

A. Listen to these sentences. Draw an arrow pointing down if the voice falls at the end. Draw an arrow pointing up if the voice rises at the end.

1. Would you like to go out for dinner tonight? ↗

2. What are you doing on New Year's Eve? ↘

3. How much did you spend on the birthday gift? ↘

4. What great weather we're having! ↘

5. Is Halloween next week? ↗

6. Are you going to a Halloween party?

7. I'm going to a party.

8. It's the week after next. ↘

9. No thanks, I'm working. ↘

10. It's too good to be true. ↘

11. Over a hundred dollars. ↘

12. Yes. I need your help to make a costume. *opp* ↗

B. Check your answers with a partner or the class.

C. Listen again and repeat each sentence.

PRONUNCIATION ACTIVITY 8

Work with a partner to make the sentences in Pronunciation Activity 7
into conversations. Practise saying them.
Example:

Person A: Would you like to go out for dinner tonight?

Person B: No thanks, I'm working.

PRONUNCIATION ACTIVITY 9

A. Listen to the conversation. All the sentences have falling intonation.    **Track 67**

Person A: What's your favourite holiday?

Person B: It's Christmas. What about you?

Person A: My favourite holiday is Halloween.

B. Work with a partner to make similar conversations about the topics
below.   *what is your favorite day of the week*

1. favourite month of the year ↗

2. favourite season ↘

3. favourite holiday in the summer ↘

4. favourite place in this city ↗

5. favourite place to visit on vacation ↘

6. favourite way to spend New Year's Eve ↗

7. favourite sport ↘

8. favourite kind of music ↘

PRONUNCIATION ACTIVITY 10

A. Listen to the weather report and fill in the blanks.    **Track 68**

This is the world weather forecast for the 13th of _____
for the following cities:

City	High	Low	Comment
_____ City	25		fine
Beijing		–4	
Atlanta		–5	
	+1		
		3	
_____ York		–2	_____ rain
Seattle			cloudy with _____
Macau		23	_____ and warm
		27	_____ and sunny
	6		
Rio de Janeiro			

B. Work with a partner to check your work. Then read the report to your partner.

COMMUNICATING IN THE REAL WORLD

Speaking STRATEGY

If you look for and find opportunities to practise your English outside the class, your listening and speaking will get better.

A. Use your English to talk to people outside your classroom. On your own or with a partner, talk to five people outside your class. Ask them the questions below and record the information. Make a short report to the class about what you learned.

Before you begin, say this:

> May I ask you some questions? This is an assignment for my English class.

1. What's your favourite holiday? Why do you like it?

2. What do you do to celebrate this holiday?

3. Some people say we don't have enough holidays. Do you agree? If we could have another holiday, when would you like to have it, and what should we do to celebrate?

4. How did you spend last New Year's Eve? How are you going to spend next New Year's Eve?

5. What month and what season is your birthday in? What do you usually do to celebrate?

6. Could you make a prediction about the future? What do you think this city will be like in 2050?

B. Project: By yourself, or with a partner, research My Giving Moment and go to its website.

Read about and discuss some possible gifts. Make a short presentation about five gifts that you think are interesting and explain why you chose them. Who would you give these gifts to?

SELF-EVALUATION

Think about your work in this chapter. For each row in the chart sections Grammar and Language Functions, Learning Strategies, and Pronunciation, give yourself a score based on the rating scale below and write a comment in the Notes section.

Show the chart to your teacher. Talk about what you need to do to make your English better.

Rating Scale

1	2	3	4	5

Needs improvement. ← ――――――――――――――――――→ *Great!*

	Score	Notes
Grammar and Language Functions		
talking about holidays and celebrations		
asking for and giving information about the seasons and weather		
asking about and expressing future plans and intentions		
making predictions about the future		
making and responding to invitations		
Pronunciation		
recognizing and pronouncing the vowels /a/ and /ow/		
using falling intonation with statements, commands, and *wh-* questions		
Learning Strategies		
Speaking		
looking for and finding opportunities to practise English outside the class		

Listening		
checking my progress and trying to find out why I don't understand sometimes		
summarizing the information I hear to improve my understanding		

Vocabulary and Language Chunks

Look at this list of new vocabulary and language chunks you learned in this chapter. Give yourself a score based on the rating scale and write a comment.

all over	to get rid of	to get ready
around the world	to stand for	on a mission
to have parties	to make a resolution	a herd of
to crowd into	to save up	take along
to make a wish	to head straight to	to feed oneself
for good luck	word gets around	apiece
to clean up	to pay one's own way	a bit
to go on a picnic	plenty of	a love affair

	Score	Notes
understanding new vocabulary and language chunks		
using new words and phrases correctly		

Write six sentences and use new vocabulary you learned in this chapter.

1. _____

2. _____

3. _____

4. _____

5. _____

6. _____

My plan for practising is _____

_____

_____

_____

CHAPTER 7

Keeping in Shape
Health and Fitness

Asking for and giving advice

Expressing necessity

Making suggestions

Expressing necessity in the past

THINKING AND TALKING

Do this fitness survey. Then work with a partner to compare your survey. Talk about some bad habits each of you would like to change.

1. Do you smoke?   YES   NO   If YES, how many cigarettes per day? _____
2. Do you drink alcohol?   YES   NO   If YES, how much? _____
3. How many hours do you sleep per night? _____
4. What's your stress level from 1 to 10? _____ (1 = very low, 10 = very high)
5. Are you overweight? _____ Were you overweight as a child? _____
6. Rate your fitness level from 1 to 10 _____ (1 = worst, 10 = best)
7. Do you play sports?   YES   NO   If YES, how often? _____
8. How often do you do fitness activities?

Circle one. 7 times per week, 3–4 times per week, 1–2 times per week, 0 times per week

9. Do you eat breakfast?   YES   NO   If YES, how often? _____
10. Do you eat junk food?   YES   NO   If YES, how often? _____
11. Do you eat late at night? YES   NO   If YES, how often? _____
12. Do you take vitamins?   YES   NO   If YES, which ones? _____
13. How many glasses of water do you drink per day? _____
14. Describe your overall health and fitness. _____

ii SPEAKING ACTIVITY 1

Work with a partner. Describe two bad habits you have and ask your partner what you should do.

My Bad Habits	My Partner's Advice

SPEAKING 1

Communication Focus 1: Asking For and Giving Advice

We use *should* to give advice or to say that something is a good idea. When we say someone *should* do something, we mean that it's a good idea, but the person can choose to do it or not. It isn't necessary.
Examples:

Affirmative	Negative	Question Forms
She should go on a diet.	She shouldn't eat a lot candy.	Should she stop smoking?
They should study more.	They shouldn't stay up late.	Why should they use dictionaries?
You should exercise if you want to lose weight.	You shouldn't eat junk food.	Should you eat bread?

SPEAKING ACTIVITY 2

Speaking STRATEGY

If you make your learning personal by applying new learning to your own life and your own situation, you will be able to express yourself better and remember the new things you have learned.

Swimming

yoga

Gym exercises

Plaiming

A. Work with a partner and label the activities in the pictures. Use the vocabulary list on the next page.

B. These activities can improve your health and fitness. Please circle all the activities that interest you. Then compare with your partner. Give each other some advice about where you can do the activities.

aerobics	fitness classes	cycling	soccer	basketball
tennis	volleyball	ice skating	yoga	golf
individual personal training	skiing	hiking	swimming	rock climbing

👥 SPEAKING ACTIVITY 3

Work with a partner. Discuss the following questions and report to the class.

1. Do the people in your home country exercise more or less often than the people in other countries? Why do you think that is?

2. What is the favourite sport in your home country? What sports do you think North Americans and Canadians like the best?

3. What exercise or sport do you do regularly? Explain why you like it.

4. Is there a particular sport or activity that you like to do in the spring or summer?

5. What sport or activity would you like to take up if you could afford it?

6. Have you ever watched a game or sports activity at a large stadium? If so, describe what it was like.

7. What sports activities do you watch on TV? Explain why.

👥 SPEAKING ACTIVITY 4

A. Work with a partner. What should people do if they have the following health problems? Make sentences using *should*. Choose from the advice section below.

Problems

have a headache	have a cough	have a sore throat
have a fever	have a backache	have a toothache
have an earache	have a stomach ache	have a sore ankle
have itchy skin	have a cold	have a burn

Advice

Take vitamin C.	Put some lotion on it.	Drink lots of liquids.
Go to bed and rest.	Take some aspirin.	Put a heating pad on it.
Put some ice on it.	See the dentist.	Take some cough syrup.
Get some ear drops.	See the doctor.	Gargle with salt water.
Stay off your legs.	Take something to settle your stomach.	

1. **If you have a headache, you should take some aspirin.**
2. If you have a fever, you should see the doctor.
3. If you have a earache, you should get some ear drops.
4. If you have itchy skin, you should put some lotion on it.
5. If you have a cough, you should take some cough syrup.
6. If you have a backache, you should put a heating pad on it.
7. If you have a stomach ache, you should take something to settle your stomach.
8. If you have a cold, you should take vitamine E and drink lots of liquids.
9. If you have a sore throat, you should gargle with salt water
10. If you have a toothache, you should see the dentist.
11. If you have a sore ankle, you should stay off your legs.
12. If you have a burn, you should put some lotion it.

B. Check your answers with another pair.

SPEAKING ACTIVITY 5

Work with a partner. Brainstorm answers to the following questions.
Then join another pair of students and compare your answers.

What should students do?

1. **Students should come to class on time.**
2. Students should do homework
3. Students should pay attention.
4. Students should study very hard.

What shouldn't students do?

1. **Students shouldn't come to class late.**
2. Student shouldn't be later.
3. Student shouldn't leave the class before finishing.
4. Student shouldn't cheat.

What should teachers do?

1. **Teachers should be fair to all the students.**
2. Teachers should make lesson plans.
3. Teachers should explain very well.
4. Teachers should be clear.

What shouldn't teachers do?

1. **Teachers shouldn't give surprise tests.**
2. Teachers shouldn't hurt students.

3. _Teachers shouldn't give special._
4. _Teachers shouldn't to special students._

What should parents do?

1. **Parents should take care of their children.**
2. _Parents should teach their children good manners and right conduc_
3. _Parents should develop communication with their kids._
4. _Parents should collaborative with their kids education._

What shouldn't parents do?

1. **Parents shouldn't spoil their children.**
2. _Parents shouldn't abandon their children education._
3. _Parents shouldn't teach racist ideas._
4. _Parents shouldn't discourage their kids about school._

SPEAKING ACTIVITY 6

Practise the dialogue with a partner.

Person A: I have a big problem. I am putting on weight. What should I do? Can you give me some advice?

Person B: I don't know. Maybe you should keep a food diary to see if you are eating too much.

Person A: Okay, thanks. That's a good idea. I'll try it.

Person B: Oh, and you shouldn't eat too many snacks with sugar in them.

Now match the advice to the problem. Then make up dialogues using *should* and *shouldn't* for each problem listed.

Problems

I'm out of shape. 5

Going to fitness classes is boring. 7

I'm tired all the time. 5

I sleep less than six hours every night. 4

I eat junk food all the time because I can't cook. 1

I'm overweight. 2

I don't have any friends. 6

Advice

1. Take a cooking course.
2. Get a physical checkup.
3. Go on a diet and do exercises.
4. Go to bed at the same time every night.
5. Go to fitness classes with friends.
6. Join some after school clubs.
7. Start an exercise program and stick to it.

SPEAKING ACTIVITY 7

Make a quick chart with the headings shown below. Walk around the room and talk to as many people as you can. Tell each person about a big problem you have. Ask that person for advice. Write down the names of the people you talked to and the advice they gave you.

Example:

> Problem: I have a big problem. I can't sleep at night. What should I do?
>
> Advice: Maybe you should keep your bedroom dark and cool. That should help.

I have a problem. My problem is _____

What should I do?

Name	Advice

LISTENING 1

Before You Listen

PRE-LISTENING ACTIVITY

Work in groups. Brainstorm some of the ways that college students may be different from other people in their families. What kinds of difficulties can this cause? Report your ideas to the class.

PRE-LISTENING VOCABULARY

You will hear a conversation on the audio CD that includes the following words. Work with a partner or by yourself to find the definition of each word.

beer	vegan *chevoco*	opposite *mejoray*	perfect	appearance *aparcncio*
drama	checkup	to improve	to socialize	broomstick → *palo de escoba*
physical	conscious *consciente*	stress	to complain → *quejarse*	

Definitions	Vocabulary
1. an alcoholic drink made from malt or grains	*beer*
2. ideal; the best; having nothing wrong → *nada malo*	*perfect*
3. the way someone or something looks	*appearence*

continued on next page

Definitions	Vocabulary
4. to interact, mix, be friendly with	socialize
5. having to do with the body, not the mind	physical
6. a story performed on stage; a play	drama
7. being awake and able to understand where you are; being aware	conscious
8. mental or emotional pressure; tension or worry	stress
9. completely different; unlike	opposite
10. to get better	to improve
11. a person who does not eat or use any animal products	vegan
12. an examination	checkup
13. to say you are unhappy or uncomfortable about a situation	to complain
14. the long handle of a broom, which is a tool we use to sweep the floor	broomstick

Choose the correct words from the list to fill in the blanks in these sentences. Use each word only once. Not all the words are used in the sentences. Please make changes to verbs or nouns when necessary.

1. I have a busy schedule, but my sister is the __opposite__. She has tons of free time.

2. Jason wants to be an actor, so he took a __drama__ course last semester.

3. Anna doesn't make any grammar mistakes. She speaks __perfect__ English.

4. My sister wants to look pretty. She always worries about her __appearance__.

5. You need to see the doctor for a __physical__ __checkup__ once a year.

6. Nina wants to get better at playing computer games. She wants to __improve__.

7. My sister doesn't eat meat or animal products of any kind. She's a __vegan__.

8. Allen has a very busy life. He feels a lot of __stress__ and doesn't have time to __socialize__ with people.

9. Erika takes a lot of vitamins because she is very health __conscious__.

Listening for the Main Ideas

Listen to the conversation and answer the questions. *They are talking about their siblings.* 🎧 **Track 69**

1. What is this conversation about? *They are worried about their siblings*
2. Why are they talking about this? *Diet/food studies.*
3. What are three problems they are discussing? *Habits, managing times Apperance, health*
4. What do you think will happen after this conversation? *They are going to have coffee.*

Listening Comprehension

Listen to the conversation as many times as necessary and answer the questions. 🎧 **Track 70**

1. Where are Nina's sister and John's brother?

   They are away at university.

2. What's the matter with Allen's diet? What shouldn't he do?
   Too much junk food and beer. He shouldn't drink to much beer.
   que pasa   con la diet

3. What's the matter with Erika's diet? What shouldn't she do?
   Always on a diet. She isn't eating properly → apropiado

4. What should Allen do about his appearance?
   He should try to take care of himself.

5. What shouldn't Erika do about her appearance?
   She shouldn't exercise too much.

6. What's the difference between Erika and Allen in their social lives?
   Allen has no social life, but Erika is very busy in her social life.

7. What should Erika do about her social life?
   Erika should reduce her social life./more time for family.

8. What should Allen do about his social life?
   He should spend less times playing games/more time with family.

9. What is the same about Allen and Erika?
   The both lack equilibrium

10. What do Nina and John decide they should do?
    Relax / don't worry / go for coffee.

Personalizing

Work with a partner. Tell each other about someone you know who has some problems or who is difficult to get along with or to understand. Discuss what advice you want to give that person.

What kind of problems do students in other countries have? How are they similar to or different from college students here?

Vocabulary and Language Chunks

Write the number of the expression next to the meaning. After checking your answers, choose five expressions and write your own sentences.

Words and Expressions	Meanings
1. to be away	__1__ not present, in another place
2. to put on weight	__13__ to become thinner and to weigh less
3. on a diet	__2__ to become heavier, to weigh more
4. to feel sorry for	__12__ to take care of
5. to care about	__11__ to have a physical examination
6. to make friends	__10__ to set up a time to meet
7. tons of	__9__ an expression we use when we want to bring up another, opposite idea
8. to be stressed out	__7__ a lot of
9. on the other hand	__6__ to form friendships
10. to make an appointment	__8__ to feel a very high level of pressure or stress
11. to get a checkup	__5__ to feel concern or worry about, to have feelings for
12. to look after	__4__ to feel sadness or pity for
13. to lose weight	__3__ eating certain foods to lose weight
14. to make time	__14__ to find the time to do something

👥 SPEAKING ACTIVITY 8

Read "Health and Wellness Tips" on the next page with a partner and together decide which three tips are the most important for students at your school. Report to the class.

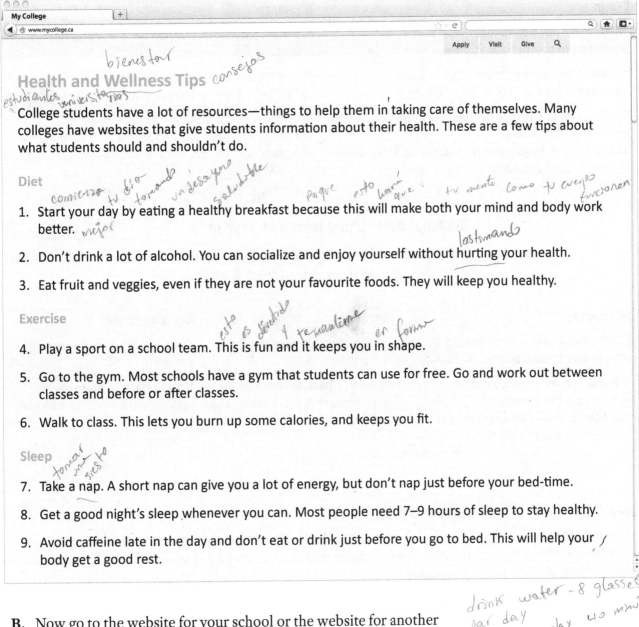

Health and Wellness Tips

College students have a lot of resources—things to help them in taking care of themselves. Many colleges have websites that give students information about their health. These are a few tips about what students should and shouldn't do.

Diet

1. Start your day by eating a healthy breakfast because this will make both your mind and body work better.

2. Don't drink a lot of alcohol. You can socialize and enjoy yourself without hurting your health.

3. Eat fruit and veggies, even if they are not your favourite foods. They will keep you healthy.

Exercise

4. Play a sport on a school team. This is fun and it keeps you in shape.

5. Go to the gym. Most schools have a gym that students can use for free. Go and work out between classes and before or after classes.

6. Walk to class. This lets you burn up some calories, and keeps you fit.

Sleep

7. Take a nap. A short nap can give you a lot of energy, but don't nap just before your bed-time.

8. Get a good night's sleep whenever you can. Most people need 7–9 hours of sleep to stay healthy.

9. Avoid caffeine late in the day and don't eat or drink just before you go to bed. This will help your body get a good rest.

B. Now go to the website for your school or the website for another college or university and find three other health and wellness tips that are important. Present your ideas to the class.

SPEAKING 2

Communication Focus 2: Expressing Necessity

When we want to say that something is necessary, we can use *must* + the base form of the verb. Another way of expressing necessity is to use *have to* + the base form of the verb. *Must* is more formal than *have to,* but it has the same meaning.

Examples	Meanings
Sarah **must pay** her school fees. Sarah **has to pay** her school fees.	It's necessary for her to pay her fees. She has no choice.
You **must be** over 16 to get a driver's licence. You **have to be** over 16 to get a driver's licence.	It's necessary for a person to be more than 16 years old to get a driver's licence. You have no choice.
Students **must get** over 60 percent in this course to pass to the next class. Students **have to get** over 60 percent in this course to pass to the next class.	It's necessary for students to get more than 60 percent to pass to the next class. If they get less than 60 percent, they will not pass.

Grammar Note: Using *must* and *have to*

Both *must* and *have to* express necessity, but note that in the negative and when asking questions, we only use *have to*.

Affirmative	Negative	Question Forms
Sandra **must take** all the antibiotics. Sandra **has to take** all the antibiotics.	Sandra **doesn't have to take** all the antibiotics.	**Does** Sandra **have to take** all the antibiotics?
You **must make** an appointment if you want to see the dentist. You **have to make** an appointment if you want to see the dentist.	You **don't have to make** an appointment if you want to see the dentist.	**Do** you **have to make** an appointment if you want to see the dentist?

Speaking STRATEGY

When you are speaking, apply the grammar rules that you are learning to express yourself more clearly and accurately.

SPEAKING ACTIVITY 9

Work with a partner. These are actions that people must do to stay healthy. Restate them with *have to* and add *but* and a negative statement.
Example:

People must sleep.

People have to sleep but they don't have to sleep 12 hours a day.

1. People must eat.

   People must eat, but they don't have to eat 6 times a day.

2. People must drink.

   People must drink, but they don't have to drink alcohol.

3. People must wear clothes.

   People must wear clothes, but they don't need to wear to many clothes.

4. People must breathe.

   People must breathe, but they don't have to breathe dirty air.

5. People must wash.

People must wash, but they don't have to 20 times a day.

6. People must look after their children.

People must look after their children, but they don't have to look after their children driving.

7. People must move around.

People must move around, but they don't have to move all the time.

8. Something else that is necessary:

People have to complete their sentences, but they have to use correct grammar.

👥 SPEAKING ACTIVITY 10

Work with a partner. Discuss the questions below and then report to the class.

Example:

What are two things people must do if they want to take this English class? What is one thing they should do?

1. They have to register.
2. They have to pay a fee.
3. They should study hard.

A. What are two things people have to do if they want to drive in this city? What is one thing they should do?

1. _They have to register their car._
2. _They have to get a driver licence_
3. _They should driving friendly_ (poseen)

B. What are two things people have to do if they own a dog? What is one thing they should do?

1. _They have to register their dog._
2. _They have to take him to the vet for vaccinations._
3. _They should walking their dog every day.) They should clean their dog._

C. What are two things people must do if they live in a house? What is one thing they should do?

1. _They have to pay the rent and the services._
2. _They have to respect their neighbours._
3. _They should clean their house._

D. What are two things people must do in this city if they want to get married? What is one thing they should do?

1. _They have to go to registry._
2. _They have to present the necessary documents for the ceremoy_
3. _They should invite their family and friends._

SPEAKING ACTIVITY 11

A. Make a quick chart with the headings shown below. Walk around the room and talk to the other people in your class. Find out and record the answers to these questions. Report the most interesting answers to the class.

Names	What are two things you have to do this week?	What don't you have to do this week?

B. Write about two students you talked to.

SPEAKING ACTIVITY 12

In this activity, you are looking for 12 people. Walk around the room and speak to as many classmates as you need to, to find the following people and write their names on the chart.

Find someone who has to go to the bank this week. Question: **Do you have to go to the bank this week?** Name:	Find someone who has to buy groceries today. Question: Name:	Find someone who has to pay bills this week. Question: Name:
Find someone who has to study for a test. Question: Name:	Find someone who has to clean up his/her room this week. Question: Name:	Find someone who has to go to an appointment this week. Question: Name:
Find someone who has to buy some clothes this week. Question: Name:	Find someone who has to do the laundry this week. Question: Name:	Find someone who has to go to the drugstore this week. Question: Name:

Find someone who has to go to the library this week. Question: Name:	Find someone who has to send some emails today. Question: Name:	Find someone who has to make a long-distance call this week. Question: Name:

᚛ SPEAKING ACTIVITY 13

Work with a partner. Look at the actions below. Decide which actions are necessary and which are simply a good idea for students. Then join another pair of students and compare your answers.

pay fees	**Students must pay fees.**
study hard	**Students should study hard.**
eat three meals a day	Students should eat three times a day
talk to their parents	should talk to their parents.
eat	have to eat
drink	have to drink
sleep	have to sleep
make friends	should make friends
go to the library	should to the library
take exams	have to take exam
wear clothes	have to wear clothes
work in study groups	should work in study groups
breathe	have to breathe
socialize with others students	Should socialize with others students

᚛ SPEAKING ACTIVITY 14

Work with a partner. Decide which actions are

- not necessary and students don't have to do them
- not advisable or not a good idea for students

Join another pair of students and compare your answers.

clean up the classroom	Students don't have to clean up the classroom. It's not necessary.
tell lies	Students shouldn't tell lies. It's not a good idea.
come to class late	shouldn't come to class late.
skip school	shouldn't skip school.
give the teacher presents	don't have to give the teacher present.
cheat on tests	students shouldn't cheat on tests.
mark tests	students don't have to mark test
take attendance	
speak their first language in class	students shouldn't speak their first language in class
explain grammar	don't have to
stay out late on school nights	shouldn't
pay to get a library card	don't have to
pay to use the school gym	don't have to
stay at school all day	don't have to

Communication Focus 3: Making Suggestions

We use *should* and some other expressions to make suggestions. *Should* is a strong way of making a suggestion.

Expressions for Suggesting	Example
Why don't you . . .	**Why don't you** take an aspirin if you have a headache?
Why not . . .	**Why not** take an aspirin if you have a headache?
It's a good idea . . .	**It's a good idea** to take an aspirin if you have a headache.
You should . . .	**You should** take an aspirin if you have a headache.

👥 SPEAKING ACTIVITY 15

Complete the dialogues with a partner and then practise saying them. Then make up your own dialogue.

1. Person A: I have a huge problem. My best friend invited me to her birthday party tonight.

    Person B: That's not a problem. You'll have a great time.

    Person A: But I have a mid-term test tomorrow and I have to study. What should I do?

    Person B: _You should go only short time!_

2. Person A: I'm in trouble. My boss wants me to work tonight.

    Person B: What's wrong with that? You'll make some extra money.

Person A: But my mother has a medical test and I have to take her to the hospital. What should I do?

Person B: _You should talk to your boss, he should understand your situation._

3. Person A: I've got a big problem. I bought a car last week from my friend.

Person B: That's okay. You don't have to take the bus any more.

Person A: The car broke down and I have to fix it but I spent all my money buying it. What should I do?

Person B: _You should talk to your friends for help you._

4. Person A: I need your help. I took the subway home yesterday.

Person B: What happened?

Person A: I found a bag with $10,000 in it on the train and I took it home. What should I do?

Person B: _You should to reparte at the subway._

5. Person A: I don't know what to do. My girlfriend loves cats and asked me to babysit her two cats when she goes away for two weeks

Person B: Why what's the matter with that? It's only for two weeks.

Person A: Yes, but I'm allergic to cats. They make me very sick, but if I don't babysit them she'll be really mad. What should I do?

Person B: _You should talk about her._

Communication Focus 4: Expressing Necessity in the Past

When we want to say that something was necessary in the past, we use *had to* + the base form of the verb.

Examples	Meanings
Sarah **had to pay** her school fees last week.	It was necessary for her to pay her fees. She had no choice and she did it.
The students **had to get** over 60 percent last semester to pass.	It was necessary for students to get more than 60 percent last semester to pass. They got over 60 percent and passed.

Grammar Note: Using *had to*—Expressing Necessity in the Past

Affirmative	Negative	Question Forms
Sandra **had to take** all the antibiotics.	Sandra **didn't have to take** all the antibiotics.	**Did** Sandra **have to take** all the antibiotics?

👥 SPEAKING ACTIVITY 16

A. Fill in the blanks in the story below using verbs from the list. You may use verbs more than once. Use either the affirmative or negative forms of *had to*.

A Trip to China

book	exchange	learn	consult	make	see
get	find out	take	call	worry	

A year ago Emily and Catherine visited China. They **had to get visas** before they left and they _had to make_ sure their passports were in order. They also _had to see_ the doctor and they _had to get_ some shots. They _had to consult_ their travel agent about their plans. They _had to book_ their flights and they _had to find out_ hotel reservations. They ___take___ their cellphones because ___call___ their parents every day. They ___exchage___ some Chinese money but they _didn't have to take_ a lot of money because they were able to use their bank cards in China. They were glad that they _didn't had to learn_ Chinese because it's a difficult language, and there are so many people who speak English in China. They only ___learn___ how to say "hello." They also _didn't had to worry_ about what to do there because there are so many things to see and do in China.

shots = inyecciones

didn't had to learn ?

B. Compare your answers with a partner.

👥 SPEAKING ACTIVITY 17

Work with a partner. Tell each other five things you had to do before you came to this city.

Me	My Partner
I had to get a passport before I came here.	I had to rent a house.
I had to get a visa.	
I had to make a plan.	
I had to book a ticket.	
I had to catch my flight on time.	

👥👥 SPEAKING ACTIVITY 18

Work in groups of three. Find out three things you each had to do when you were children, and three things you didn't have to do. Use the chart on the next page. Report to the class.

Name	What did you have to do when you were a child?	What didn't you have to do?
Partner 1	1. I did go to school every day 2. I 3.	I didn't have to go alone. I didn't have to driving a car.
Partner 2	1. 2. 3.	
Me	1. I did make my homework every day. 2. I did to clean my room on the weekend. 3. I had to listen to my mother	I didn't have to stay alone on the street. -I didn't have to cook.

LISTENING 2

Before You Listen

👥 **PRE-LISTENING ACTIVITY**

Work with a partner. Organize the five paragraphs below to tell a story. Check your work with the class. Then answer the questions.

    4   a. Michelle won many wheelchair races. In 2011, Michelle won three gold medals and a silver medal at the World Championships in New Zealand. Michelle made history at the London 2012 Paralympic Games when she won the 200 m race and won the silver medal in the 100 m race. In July 2013 she again won the championship in Lyons, France, and she continued training for the Paralympic Games.

    1   b. When Michelle Stilwell was 17 years old she was riding piggyback with a friend and she had a terrible accident. She fell down a long flight of stairs.

    5   c. These days, Michelle has a very busy schedule—she is married, she is a full-time mother, and in 2013, the people of British Columbia elected her to be a member of the provincial legislative assembly. She says "anything is possible with a positive attitude."

    3   d. Michelle's first sport was wheelchair basketball, but her injury made it difficult for her to play this sport. Michelle didn't give up. She changed to a new sport—she became a wheelchair racer. She became world champion in just two years.

    2   e. Michelle injured her spinal cord and could not walk. She became a quadriplegic. Before this Michelle loved sports and was an excellent athlete. Her injury did not stop her, but she had to make some changes. She started playing parasports—sports for people who have a disability.

Michelle's Story

1. (b) When Michelle Stilwell was 17 years old she was riding piggyback with a friend, and she had a terrible accident. She fell down a long flight of stairs.

2. _Michelle won many wheelchair races._

3. _In 2011, Michelle won three gold medals._

4. _____

5. _____

1. What caused Michelle's injury?

   _____

2. What was the first sport for people with disabilities that Michelle played?

   _____

3. Why did she have to change sports?

   _____

4. Why did she make history in London in 2012?

   _____

5. How many occupations does Michelle have?

   _____

6. What is her motto?

   _____

PRE-LISTENING VOCABULARY

You will hear a recording on the audio CD that includes the following words. Work with a partner or by yourself to find the definition of each word.

disability _discapacidad_	Paralympics	curling	able-bodied
event _evento_	awareness	to perceive	shift
progression	power	competitive	achievement
to participate	recruitment	wheelchair	campaign
occupational therapy	sled hockey		

Definitions	Vocabulary
1. international sports contests for people with disabilities held after the summer and winter Olympics	Paralympics
2. anything that puts a person at a disadvantage, usually physical or mental	disability
3. knowing about; understanding; being aware of	awareness
4. a game played on the ice with large flat stones and brooms	curling
5. a special chair with large wheels designed for people who have difficulty walking	wheelchair
6. hockey played from a sled	sled hockey
7. healthy; not physically disabled	able-body
8. a planned activity; something that happens	event
9. ability or strength to do something	power
10. to see; to become aware of; to understand	to perceive
11. a change	shift
12. development or progress	progression
13. characterized by competition	competitive
14. training to teach people to do the activities of everyday living after they have had physical injuries	ocupational therapy
15. actions or organized work to reach a goal	campaing
16. accomplishment; something important a person has done	achievement
17. to take part in	to participate
18. the work of finding and getting people to take part in something, such as sports	recruitment

Choose the correct words from the list above to fill in the blanks in these sentences. Use each word only once. Not all the words are used in the sentences. Please make changes to verbs or nouns when necessary.

1. Athletes with disabilities compete at the __Paralympics__ which take place after the summer and winter Olympics.

2. Michelle Stilwell doesn't let her __disability__ stop her from living a normal life.

3. The best _able - body_ athletes _participate_ in the Olympic Games every four years.

4. Children with _disabilities_ can't play hockey but they can play _sled hockey_ in the winter.

5. Winning the gold medal was a wonderful _achievement_.

6. We are going to the Paralympic Games. We want to get tickets for all the _events_.

7. Michelle Stilwell's athletic performance raised many people's _awareness_ about parasports or sports for people with disabilities.

8. Michelle loves to compete in races and other sports. She's very _competitive_.

9. The government wanted more disabled people to participate in sports. It started a _recruitment_ _campaing_ to get these people involved in sports.

10. Michelle is a very strong person. She has the _____ to win races and to get people involved in sports.

Listening STRATEGY 🎧

When you are listening to an interview or report, try to find out the main idea and the purpose of the report. This will help you understand.

Listening for the Main Ideas

Track 71

Listen to the report and underline the best answer for each question.

1. What is this interview about?
   a. athletes and sports
   b. the medals Michelle Stilwell won
   c. the development of Paralympic sports

2. What is the purpose of this news program?
   a. to teach children about winter sports
   b. to get more disabled people involved in sports
   c. to explain parasports or sports for disabled people

Listening Comprehension

Track 72

Listen to the report as many times as necessary. Write *T* if the statement is true or *F* if it is false.

1. Michelle Stilwell won the gold medal only in wheelchair basketball. _F_

2. This report happened on the UN International Day of Persons with Disabilities. _T_

3. Michelle Stilwell teaches able-bodied children to play wheelchair sports. _T_

5. Michelle Stilwell is glad that more people are learning about disabled athletes. _T_

6. Michelle doesn't think that life is better for athletes with disabilities today. _____F_____

7. Michelle says that competitive sports for athletes with disabilities have not changed very much. _____F_____

8. Michelle got interested in playing sports for disabled people when she was still in the hospital. _____T_____

9. Michelle won four gold medals and one silver medal. _____T_____

10. Training for the Paralympics is now a full-time job for athletes with disabilities. _____T_____

11. Thirteen percent of Canadians with disabilities participate in sport. _____F_____

12. The hospital let Michelle leave for one day to watch a wheelchair basketball game. _____T_____

13. The Canadian Paralympic ~~Committee~~ *comité* wants more people with disabilities to play sports. _____T_____

Personalizing

1. Work with a partner. Decide which three Olympic or Paralympic sports events you think are the most exciting to watch. Explain why. Then join another pair of students and share your opinions. Report to the class.

2. Michelle Stilwell says that she believes anything is possible with a positive attitude. Do you agree? Explain and give examples to support your ideas. *Yes, I believe that everything you set out to do in life, if you try hard you can achieve it. -> If you believe you can.*

Vocabulary and Language Chunks

Write the number of the expression next to the meaning. After checking your answers, choose five expressions and write your own sentences.

Words and Expressions

1. track and field
   atletismo

2. gold medallist

3. to spread the word
   Para correr la voz

4. a step forward
   un paso adelante

Meanings

___8___ to examine, find out more information about something

___4___ permission to do something for a day

___1___ a variety of competitive athletic events and sports played outside in a field, such as racing, jumping, weight throwing

___2___ a person who won a gold medal

5. full time   _____6_____ to succeed even with very few chances
6. to defy the odds   _____3_____ to tell information to many people
7. day pass   _____5_____ working the full number of hours considered normal for a day's work
8. to check it out   _____4_____ an improvement; a change for the better

PRONUNCIATION

Pronunciation Focus 1: The /θ/ Sound

Track 73

We make the /θ/ sound by putting the tongue beneath the upper front teeth and blowing air out of the mouth. Repeat these words with the /θ/ sound:

Thursday, think, thanks, bath, math, birthday

PRONUNCIATION ACTIVITY 1

Listen to the pairs of words. Circle *same* if the words sound the same and *different* if the words sound different.

1. same / different
2. same / different
3. same / different
4. same / different
5. same / different

6. same / different
7. same / different
8. same / different
9. same / different
10. same / different

PRONUNCIATION ACTIVITY 2

Track 74

A. Listen to each sentence and then repeat it.
B. Listen again and write the sentence.

1. That your math book.
2. Are you both getting together in thanksgiving?
3. where's the ticket both for the boat ride?
4. what does math mean?
5. how do you spelle fourth?
6. It's on the ten on the months
7. They threw that thing on the mat.

C. Work with a partner and write the missing sentences in these dialogues below, using the sentences you have written in Part B. Then practise saying them.

1. a. <u>What does *math* mean?</u>

    b. It's the study of numbers and their relationships.

2. a. When is our math test?

    b. _____

3. a. _____

    b. Yes. We're having dinner at my mother's.

4. a. _____

    b. It's next to the boat docks.

5. a. What did the children do with the bird's nest?

    b. _____

6. a. _____

    b. F-O-U-R-T-H

Pronunciation Focus 2: The /ð/ Sound

We make the /ð/ sound by putting the tongue beneath the upper front teeth, blowing air out of the mouth, and making a vibrating sound in the throat. Repeat these words with the /ð/ sound:

 **Track 75**

this, there, breathe, weather, further

PRONUNCIATION ACTIVITY 3

Listen to these pairs of words. Which word has the /ð/ sound?
Circle 1 or 2.

    a. 1   2   f. 1   2

    b. 1   2   g. 1   2

    c. 1   2   h. 1   2

    d. 1   2   i. 1   2

    e. 1   2   j. 1   2

PRONUNCIATION ACTIVITY 4

Work with a partner. Choose five words with the /θ/ sound or the /ð/ sound that you use a lot. Write five sentences with these words. Join another pair of students and dictate the sentences to them.

Pronunciation Focus 3: The Consonants /tʃ/ (ch), /dʒ/ (j or g), /ʃ/ (sh), and /ʒ/

Track 76

To make the / tʃ / sound, touch the roof of the mouth quickly with the tip of the tongue and let the air out.

Repeat these words with the / tʃ / sound:

church, watch, chips, which

To make the / dʒ / sound, touch the roof of the mouth a little further back with the tongue and make a vibrating sound in the throat as you let the air out.

Repeat these words with the / dʒ / sound:

juice, June, age, message

To make the / ʃ / sound, don't touch the roof of the mouth but bring the tip of the tongue close to it and let the air out.

Repeat these words with the / ʃ / sound:

wash, wish, shirt, fishing

To make the / ʒ / sound, bring the tongue close to the roof of the mouth but don't touch it. Let the air out while making a vibrating sound in the throat.

Repeat these words with the / ʒ / sound:

pleasure, treasure, television, usually

👥 PRONUNCIATION ACTIVITY 5

Track 77

A. Listen to these words. Repeat them and then write them.

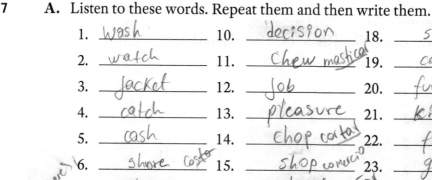

1. _wash_
2. _watch_
3. _jacket_
4. _catch_
5. _cash_
6. _shore_ Costa
7. _chores_ quehaceres
8. _college_
9. _July_
10. _decision_
11. _chew_ masticar
12. _job_
13. _pleasure_
14. _chop_ cortar
15. _shop_ comercio
16. _cheat_ engañar
17. _gym_
18. _sheets_ shojas
19. _casual_
20. _furniture_
21. _kitchen_
22. _fridge_
23. _garage_
24. _Asia_
25. _beige_

B. Work with a partner. Check your answers and then fill in the blanks in the sentences below with the correct word. Practise saying the sentences to your partner.

Example:

What does she ___watch___ on TV?

1. Don't eat so fast. You have to ___chew___ your food.

2. Please don't ___cheat___ on the test.

3. Be careful. Don't ___catch___ a cold.

4. It's a ___pleasure___ to work with you.

5. Japan and Korea are in ___Asia___.

6. We can go to the ___gym___ when we finish our ___job___.

7. Please ___wash___ the vegetables in the ___kitchen___.

8. Does she ___wash___ the bed ___sheets___? *lava las sabanas?*

9. She doesn't want to pay ___cash___ for the ___jacket___. Can she use a credit card?

10. He got a ___job___ in a ___garage___.

11. Don't put the vegetables in the ___fridge___.

12. The ___college___ closes in ___July___.

13. She made a ___decision___ to buy a ___causual___ dress for the occasion.

PRONUNCIATION ACTIVITY 6

A. Repeat each word that you hear and then write it.   Track 78

1. _____   11. _____
2. _____   12. _____
3. _____   13. _____
4. _____   14. _____
5. _____   15. _____
6. _____   16. _____
7. _____   17. _____
8. _____   18. _____
9. _____   19. _____
10. _____   20. _____

B. Work with a partner and make up five sentences using some of the words that you heard. Join another pair of students and teach them to say your sentences.

PRONUNCIATION ACTIVITY 7

Work with a partner. Choose eight words with the / ʃ /, / tʃ /, / ʤ /, or / ʒ / sound that you use a lot. Then make up five sentences with these words. Practise saying them to each other.

COMMUNICATING IN THE REAL WORLD

A. Use your English to talk to people outside your classroom. On your own or with a partner, talk to five people outside your class. Ask them the questions below and record the information. Make a short report to the class about what you learned.

Before you begin, say this:

> May I ask you some questions? This is an assignment for my English class.

1. a.   What fitness or sports activities do you do?
    b.   How often do you do these?

2. What bad or good habits do you have? What do you think you should do to improve?

3. What sports or fitness activities in this city do you recommend?

4. What do you think students should do and shouldn't do to be healthy and happy?

5. What do you think I should do to improve my English?

6. One Paralympic athlete says that she believes anything is possible with a positive attitude. Do you agree with that?

B. Work with a group to plan an orientation for new students coming to your school. The orientation will take the form of a video that you will put up on YouTube.

1. Brainstorm all the important information you want in your orientation.

2. Then brainstorm the pictures and interviews you need to go along with your information.

3. Finally, plan how to put your information and visuals together for the video.

4. Put your video up on YouTube and make a presentation to the class about the content and the process

SELF-EVALUATION

Think about your work in this chapter. For each row in the chart sections Grammar and Language Functions, Learning Strategies, and Pronunciation, give yourself a score based on the rating scale below and write a comment in the Notes section.

Show the chart to your teacher. Talk about what you need to do to make your English better.

Rating Scale

1	2	3	4	5

Needs improvement. ← → *Great!*

	Score	Notes
Grammar and Language Functions		
talking about health and fitness and sports		
asking for and giving advice		
asking for and making suggestions		
expressing necessity and lack of necessity in the present and past		
Pronunciation		
recognizing and pronouncing the consonants /ð/ and /θ/		
recognizing and pronouncing the consonants /ʃ/ (sh), /tʃ/ (ch), /dʒ/, and /ʒ/		
Learning Strategies		
Speaking		
applying the grammar rules I am learning to express my ideas clearly		
applying new learning to my life and my situation to express myself and remember the concepts		
Listening		
listening for the main idea and the purpose of a report or interview		

Vocabulary and Language Chunks

Look at this list of new vocabulary and language chunks you learned in this chapter. Give yourself a score based on the rating scale and write a comment.

to be away	tons of	to lose weight
to defy the odds	to put on weight	to be stressed out
full time	to check it out	on a diet
on the other hand	track and field	to make friends
to feel sorry for	to make an appointment	to spread the word
to look after	to care about	to get a checkup
a step forward	day pass	

	Score	Notes
understanding new vocabulary and language chunks		
using new words and phrases correctly		

Write six sentences and use new vocabulary you learned in this chapter.

1. _____
2. _____
3. _____
4. _____
5. _____
6. _____

My plan for practising is _____

_____

_____

_____

CHAPTER 8

Travel

Discovering the Wonderful World We Live In

Talking about experiences and accomplishments

Talking about actions begun in the past and continuing into the present

Describing and comparing

THINKING AND TALKING

Work with a partner. Match the names to the pictures of these famous places. Where are they? Have you visited any of these places? Number them according to which you would like to visit the most (1, 2, etc.). Tell your partner another place you would like to visit. Explain why you would like to visit it.

Niagara Falls	The Taj Mahal	The Great Wall
Paris	London	The Himalayas
Tokyo	Las Vegas	Shanghai

SPEAKING 1

Communication Focus 1:
Talking about Experiences and Accomplishments

We can use the simple present perfect tense to talk about experiences and accomplishments.

Expressions	Examples
I have + past participle	I **have visited** South America.
Have you ever . . . + past participle	**Have you** ever **been** to Shanghai?
She has + past participle	**She has won** the gold medal in skiing.

Grammar Note: Simple Present Perfect Tense

One way that we use the simple present perfect tense is to describe actions that happened in the past, but not at a specific time in the past.

With a specific past time reference, we do not use the present perfect. If we want to use a specific past time reference we have to use the simple past tense.
Examples:

I've visited Italy.	BUT	I visited Italy five **years ago**.
We've seen the Rocky Mountains.	BUT	We saw the Rocky Mountains **last year**.
They've travelled to Mexico.	BUT	They travelled to Mexico **before they visited South America**.

We often use the simple present perfect tense with *already* or *just*. We also use it with adverbs of frequency such as *always, never, rarely*, and *seldom. Ever* is used in questions and in negatives with *not*.
Examples:

We've already bought our plane tickets.

They've just met the new students.

She's always taken the train to Montreal.

I've never taken the bullet train in Japan.

Have you ever gone on a cruise?

He's rarely travelled out of the country.

These are the forms of the simple present perfect tense.

Affirmative	Contractions
I have seen the Rocky Mountains.	I've seen the Rocky Mountains.
You have flown around the world.	You've flown around the world.
She has been to Boston.	She's been to Boston.
He has climbed Mt. Everest.	He's climbed Mt. Everest.
It has snowed a lot.	It's snowed a lot.
We have visited Asia.	We've visited Asia.
They have travelled to New Zealand.	They've travelled to New Zealand.

Questions	Negatives
Have I seen the Rocky Mountains?	I haven't seen the Rocky Mountains.
Have you flown around the world?	You haven't flown around the world.
Has she been to Boston?	She hasn't been to Boston.
Has he climbed Mt. Everest?	He hasn't climbed Mt. Everest.
Has it snowed a lot?	It hasn't snowed a lot.
Have we visited Asia?	We haven't visited Asia.
Have they travelled to New Zealand?	They haven't travelled to New Zealand.

Speaking STRATEGY

Listening for similarities in place names in your first language and English can help you understand and express your ideas more easily in English. Many names are similar in all languages, but some are different.

SPEAKING ACTIVITY 1

A. Make a quick chart with the headings shown below. Walk around the room and talk to as many people as you can. Ask these questions:

How many continents have you visited?

How many countries have you been to?

How many cities have you visited?

What was your favourite place?

Report about one person.

Names	Continents	Countries	Cities	Favourite Place

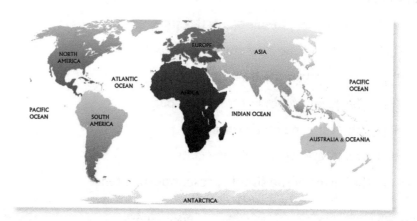

B. Write about three people in your class.
Example:

Ellen has visited two continents, three countries, and six cities. Her favourite place was Banff, Alberta.

SPEAKING ACTIVITY 2

Work with a partner. Interview your partner and find out the answers to these questions. Report to the class.

1. When you travel, what kind of trip do you prefer to take? Explain why.
   a. a trip to a city you haven't visited
   b. a trip to see natural wonders—lakes, mountains, forests
   c. a beach holiday
   d. an organized tour

2. What cities have you visited? Which city was your favourite? When did you visit it?

3. Have you ever seen any famous mountains or waterfalls? Where did you go and when did you go there?

4. What other famous sights have you visited? When did you visit them?

5. Do you prefer visiting foreign countries or travelling in your own country? Why?

6. Have you ever been afraid to travel to a place? Explain.

7. How many times have you taken a plane?

8. Have you ever hitchhiked?

9. What's your opinion of travelling? Why?

👥 SPEAKING ACTIVITY 3

A. Work with a partner. Look at the two people pictured in the chart below. Below the chart are 11 sentence endings telling about some adventures these people had. Which tell us about Marnie? Which tell us about Andrew? Discuss with your partner.

 Marnie was a world traveller many years ago. She went to Antarctica twice.	 Andrew is a travel writer and he still travels a lot. He has been to the Great Wall of China many times.

B. Circle the verb tenses in the following sentence endings, then use these to write sentences about Marnie and Andrew under the correct picture in the chart.

_____ visited a great many countries.

_____ has been to every country in Europe.

_____ travelled to the North Pole.

_____ has crossed the Sahara Desert.

_____ visited Japan and Malaysia.

_____ has always wanted to visit Greenland.

_____ lived in New Zealand for three months.

_____ has survived many travel accidents.

_____ went to Las Vegas quite a few times.

_____ wrote stories and articles about travel.

_____ has written books about travelling.

C. Check your answers with your partner. Do you agree? Which tenses are used in the sentences about Marnie? Which tenses are used in the sentences about Andrew? Talk about the difference in meaning between these two tenses.

SPEAKING ACTIVITY 4

A. Walk around the room and speak to as many people as possible. Make questions using the present perfect tense to find people who have done the activities listed below. Then find out some details, such as when they did these things.
Example:

camp in the winter

Have you ever gone camping in the winter?

When did you go camping in the winter?

Have you ever . . .

Activity	Name	When
see the northern lights		
travel in the desert		
take a cruise		
fly in a helicopter		
go bungee jumping		
be to Tokyo		
swim in the ocean		
climb a mountain		
go sky diving		
see a large waterfall		
be lost in a foreign country		
lose your passport		
miss your plane		

B. Write about four classmates.
Example:

Allen has been to Tokyo. He was there three years ago.

SPEAKING ACTIVITY 5

Work in groups of four. You have five minutes to think of and write down as many *Have you ever . . .* questions as you can. When you are finished, each of you can choose one of the questions and walk around the room to ask as many people as possible. Record the answers. Then as a group, present a report of what you found out.

Example:

> In our class, five people have gone camping in the winter. Ten students have seen a ghost . . . etc.

My Group's Questions

1. _____
2. _____
3. _____
4. _____

SPEAKING ACTIVITY 6

A. Work with a partner and fill each blank in this article with a verb from the list below. Use each verb only once.

My College   +

www.mycollege.ca

Apply   Visit   Give   Q

Michael Palin—Modern World Traveller

Michael Palin ___has made___ as a writer and actor in England, but in 1988 he

_____ travelling around the world and making documentary films about the

places he visited. He _____ documentaries and presented travel shows about

the Sahara Desert and the Himalayas. He _____ through central and eastern

Europe and recently he _____ and made a documentary about Brazil. He

_____ books about each of his trips. He _____ his books available for

people to read on his website. He _____ many awards including a gold medal

from the Royal Canadian Geographical Society.

---

has written	visited	has travelled
has made	started out	has made
has won	began	

B. Write six questions about the article.

Example:

How many countries / Michael Palin / visit

How many countries has Michael Palin visited?

1. How many documentaries / he / make

   _____ ?

2. How long ago / he / start making / documentaries

   _____ ?

3. How many books / he / write

   _____ ?

4. When / he / visit the Himalayas

   _____ ?

5. Why / he visit / so many places

   _____ ?

6. Why / he / make / his books available on his website

   _____ ?

LISTENING 1

Before You Listen

PRE-LISTENING ACTIVITY 1

Work in groups of four and answer these questions. Report the most interesting information to the class.

Questions	Me	Partner 1	Partner 2	Partner 3
What places in North America have you visited? What places would you like to visit?				
Talk about the first trip that you remember taking. Why was it memorable?				

continued on next page

Questions	Me	Partner 1	Partner 2	Partner 3
What is culture shock? Have you ever experienced it?				
Some people work as travel writers and have to travel for a living. What is your opinion of this kind of travel?				

PRE-LISTENING ACTIVITY 2

A. Work with a partner. The teacher will give you URLs for two specific websites. One partner will visit the Jim Byers website and answer these questions:

1. What is Jim Byers' job?

2. What two places did he visit recently?

The second partner will go to the Heather Greenwood Davis website and answer these questions:

1. How did the writer start travelling?

2. What two places did she visit recently?

B. Share your information with your partner and decide which website you like the best.

PRE-LISTENING VOCABULARY

A. You will hear an interview on the audio CD that includes the following words. Work with a partner or by yourself to find the definition of each word.

excursion	immensely	to spark	culture shock	to pack
locale	leisure	amazing	couple	
memorable	former	outraged	professionally	
to transform	freelance	intriguing	to explore	
rewarding	bug	frustrating	globetrotting	

Definitions	Vocabulary
1. a journey or trip for pleasure, usually short	*excursion*
2. very much; extremely; highly	
3. to cause the start of something; to start or light a fire	

continued on next page

Definitions	Vocabulary
4. state of nervousness or confusion felt by a person in a new, strange, or foreign culture	
5. a place	
6. travelling all over the world or globe	
7. to fill with things or to fill with people	
8. to change in form	
9. free time; spare time	
10. giving a reward; gratifying; satisfying; pleasing	
11. a very strong enthusiasm for something; a very strong interest in something	
12. past; previous	
13. self-employed and hired to work on different projects for different companies	
14. excellent; wonderful; so good it surprises people	
15. making a person feel angry or annoyed; irritating	
16. feeling very unhappy and very angry because of something bad, hurtful, or wrong	
17. very interesting; strange; mysterious	
18. two of something; two things or individuals	
19. to travel through or search through; to examine	
20. very interesting and easy to remember; something a person will never forget	
21. doing something as a profession or job	

B. Choose the correct words from the list above to fill in the blanks in these sentences. Use each word only once. Not all the words are used in the sentences. Please make changes to verbs or nouns when necessary.

1. When they were in Mexico on vacation, they went on several __excursions__ to visit pyramids and temples.

2. She _____ all her clothes into one suitcase when she travels.

3. The people felt _____ because the police let the criminal go free.

4. Her trip to China was wonderful. She says it was _____.

5. Could you please lend me a _____ of dollars?

6. She has been travelling all her life because she got the travel _____ when she was a teenager.

7. They are going to South America. They want to _____ as many countries as possible.

8. She has an excellent voice. She sings _____.

9. Her parents' journeys and travels _____ her interest in travelling.

10. When we went to Argentina some friends took us to some very interesting _____.

11. Anna really enjoys her work. She finds it very _____.

12. She is a travel guide now, but in her _____ job she worked in a museum.

13. They decorated the room and _____ it into a magical place.

14. Her visit to China was the most _____ trip of her life.

15. She is crazy about visiting new places. She enjoys travelling _____.

Listening for the Main Ideas

Listen to the interview and check off each answer that is correct.

Track 79

1. What kind of show is this?
    a. a travel show
    b. a call-in program with guests
    c. a program with travel writers
    d. a program about vacations

2. The purpose of this show is
    a. to find out about the guests' professions.
    b. to exchange stories about memorable travel experiences.
    c. to give people information about visiting places in North America.
    d. to give information about culture shock.

3. The host of the show asks the guests
    a. What was your most memorable travel experience?
    b. How did you get interested in travelling?
    c. Tell us about the first time you took a trip?
    d. Where would you like to go on your next vacation?

Listening Comprehension

Listen to the interview as many times as necessary. Write *T* if the statement is true or *F* if it is false.

Track 80

1. The host says that travel can change people's lives. _____

2. The host says that for some people travel is a lifestyle. _____

3. Both guests are professional travel writers. _____

4. Jim Byers and Heather Greenwood Davis both work for newspapers. _____

5. Heather's parents took their children all over Canada. _____

6. Heather and her family travelled around the world for six years. _____

7. They visited 29 countries. _____

8. When Jim's family visited Canada the American dollar and the Canadian dollar were the same value. _____

9. Jim got interested in travelling because he likes exploring new places. _____

10. Heather and her family spent 30 days in China because they can speak Mandarin. _____

11. In China people paid a lot of attention to Heather's family because they are black. _____

12. Heather and her family found travelling in China difficult and frustrating. _____

13. Heather and her family experienced culture shock in China. _____

14. Heather says that people in China helped them handle problems. _____

Personalizing

Work with a partner and answer these questions. Report or write about your partner.

1. Do you enjoy travelling? Why or why not?

2. What is your most memorable travel experience?

3. What is your worst travel experience?

4. If you could plan a trip around the world, what countries and continents would you visit? How long would you travel?

Vocabulary and Language Chunks

Write the number of the expression next to the meaning. After checking your answers, choose five expressions and write your own sentences.

Words and Expressions	Meanings
1. to get hooked on	__1__ to become addicted to; to like very, very much
2. to backpack	_____ a way of living life
3. to come to mind	_____ to change from being a young child to an adult
4. to take a toll on	_____ to visit places of interest
5. to stand out	_____ everywhere

6. to attract a crowd _____ two

7. to get through _____ to hike or travel with a knapsack carried on one's back

8. to step up _____ to get a thought or idea; to remember

9. a couple of _____ to cause difficulty, stress, or suffering

10. all over the place _____ to look different from everyone else, to be very noticeable

11. to see the sights _____ to get the attention of a large group of people

12. to grow up _____ to handle or deal with a difficult situation

13. lifestyle _____ to come forward

👥 SPEAKING ACTIVITY 7

A. Work with a partner. There are so many incredible natural sights in the world that people cannot agree about which ones should be called the seven greatest natural wonders of the world. Below is a list of some places that people have voted as natural wonders of the world. Match the names to the pictures to the right. Talk about why you think people call these wonders of the world.

Mount Everest in the Himalayas   The Grand Canyon in the USA

Rio de Janeiro Harbour in Brazil   Victoria Falls in Africa

Aurora Borealis in the Arctic regions

B. What special places in your country or province do you think deserve to be called wonders of the world?

C. Your teacher will give you a link to a website about seven natural wonders of the world.

Go to the website, click on a continent that interests you and then find a natural wonder of the world there.

Find out about it and report to the class what you have learned about this natural wonder.

SPEAKING 2

Communication Focus 2: Talking about Actions Begun in the Past and Continuing into the Present

We use the present perfect progressive tense to give and get information about actions which began in the past and are still true at the present time. We can also use the simple present perfect in this case.

We use *since* and *for* to tell how long an action has been continuing. We use *since* to tell the time **when** the action began and *for* to tell about the entire **length of time**.

Examples:

Heather <u>has been writing</u> travel stories <u>for</u> 10 years.

OR

Heather <u>has written</u> travel stories <u>for</u> 10 years.

Tourists <u>have been visiting</u> the CN Tower <u>since</u> 1976.

OR

Tourists <u>have visited</u> the CN Tower <u>since</u> 1976.

How long <u>have you been driving</u>?

OR

How long <u>have you driven</u>?

<u>I've been dreaming</u> about going to South America <u>for</u> a long time.

OR

I<u>'ve dreamed</u> about going to South America <u>for</u> a long time.

These are the forms of the present perfect progressive tense:

Affirmative	Contractions
I have been studying English for one year.	I've been studying English for one year.
You have been working for three months.	You've been working for three months.
He has been driving for two years.	He's been driving for two years.
She has been smoking for three years.	She's been smoking for three years.
It has been raining since noon.	It's been raining since noon.
We have been planning our trip since January.	We've been planning our trip since January.
They have been saving money for five years.	They've been saving money for five years.

Questions	Negatives
Have I been making mistakes?	I haven't been making mistakes.
Have you been doing your homework?	You haven't been doing your homework.
Has he been waking up early?	He hasn't been waking up early.
Has she been doing kickboxing?	She hasn't been doing kickboxing.
Has it been snowing?	It hasn't been snowing.
Have we been improving?	We haven't been improving.
Have they been waiting?	They haven't been waiting.

SPEAKING ACTIVITY 8

A. Make a quick chart with the headings shown below. Walk around the room and talk to as many classmates as possible. Find out the answers to these questions.

How long have you been speaking English?

How long have you been living in this city?

How long have you been studying at this school?

Names	Length of Time Speaking English	Length of Time Living in This City	Length of Time Studying at This School

B. Write about three classmates.
Example:

> Nina has been speaking English for one year. She has been living here for six months and she's been studying at this school for three months.

SPEAKING ACTIVITY 9

Work with a group. Answer these questions and report the most interesting information to the class.

1. What place have you been dreaming about visiting?

2. Why do you want to visit this place?

3. What have you been doing to make your dream come true?

Communication Focus 3: Describing and Comparing

We use the comparative degree of adjectives when talking about two things or people.
Examples:

> faster than, older than, bigger than.

When we talk about three or more things or people, we use the superlative degree of adjectives.
Examples:

> the fastest, the oldest, the biggest

Grammar Note: Superlatives 1

For adjectives of one syllable, add -*est* to form the superlative.
Examples:

> The <u>highest</u> mountain in the world is Mt. Everest.

> The Pacific Ocean is the <u>largest</u> in the world.

> Who is the <u>tallest</u> person in the class?

SPEAKING ACTIVITY 10

Work with a group. Answer the questions below and then report your group's answers.

Here are some expressions to use to state your opinions:

Expressions	Asking for ideas	Agreeing
I think that . . .	What do you think?	I agree
I believe that . . .	How about you?	I don't agree
I'm pretty sure that . . .		
I'm not sure but I think . . .		
In my opinion, . . .		

Questions	Answers (in complete sentences)
What is the longest river in the world?	
What is the biggest country in the world?	
What is the highest mountain in the world?	
What is the largest city in the world?	
What is the prettiest place in the world?	
What is the largest waterfall in the world?	
What is the longest mountain range?	
What is the fastest vehicle?	
What is the hardest material in the world?	
What is the hottest place in the world?	
What is the coldest place in the world?	
What is the largest animal in the world?	
What is the smartest animal?	
What is the best food in the world?	
Make your own superlative question and statement:	

Grammar Note: Superlatives 2

Adjectives of two or more syllables use *the most . . .* to form the superlative degree.

Examples:

> Who is <u>the most important</u> person in the world?

> <u>The most beautiful</u> city in Canada is Vancouver.

SPEAKING ACTIVITY 11

A. Work with a partner. Answer each question and make another sentence adding additional information.

Example:

> What is the most exciting city to live in?

> The most exciting city in the world to live in is Las Vegas because it has a lot of casinos and entertainment. Tourists come from all over the world to visit Las Vegas and they spend millions of dollars there.

1. What is the most popular travel destination in the world?

   _____

2. What is the most modern city in the world?

   _____

3. What is the most interesting country in the world to visit?

   _____

4. What is the most beautiful place in the world?

   _____

5. Who is the most important person in the world?

   _____

6. Who is the most popular entertainer in the world?

   _____

7. What is the most interesting kind of movie to watch?

   _____

8. What is the most enjoyable kind of book to read?

   _____

Speaking STRATEGY

To get more practice in speaking and making conversation, ask questions to get more information and to make your conversations last longer.

9. What is the most comfortable place to be?

_____

B. Join another pair and compare your answers. What are the similarities?

SPEAKING ACTIVITY 12

Work in groups of four and discuss these questions. Then decide on the answers. When you have finished, present your answers to the class. Does everyone agree?

Example:

Who is the (tall) _____ person in the class?

Sylvia is the tallest in the class.

1. Who is the (funny) _____ person in the class?

_____

2. Who is the (intelligent) _____ person in the class?

_____

3. Who is the (strong) _____ person in the class?

_____

4. Who is the (quiet) _____ person in the class?

_____

5. Who is the (serious) _____ person in the class?

_____

6. Who is the (old) _____ person in the class?

_____

7. Who is the (helpful) _____ person in the class?

_____

8. Who is the (outgoing) _____ person in the class?

_____

9. Who is the (creative) _____ person in the class?

_____

10. Who is the (young) _____ person in the class?

_____

11. Who is the (relaxed) _____ person in the class?

_____

12. Who is the (popular) _____ person in the class?

_____

13. Who is the (busy) _____ person in the class?

_____

14. Who is the (friendly) _____ person in the class?

_____

LISTENING 2

Before You Listen

🏃 PRE-LISTENING ACTIVITY 1

Work with a partner and read this news story. Then discuss the questions below.

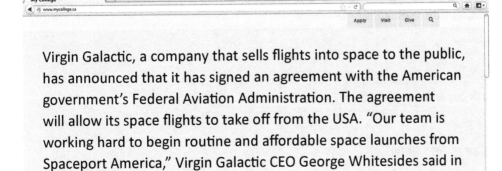

Virgin Galactic, a company that sells flights into space to the public, has announced that it has signed an agreement with the American government's Federal Aviation Administration. The agreement will allow its space flights to take off from the USA. "Our team is working hard to begin routine and affordable space launches from Spaceport America," Virgin Galactic CEO George Whitesides said in a statement.

The company plans to launch a flight in the near future. Richard Branson, the president of Virgin Galactic, plans to be on that flight.

1. Would you like to take a flight into space? Why or why not?

2. Do you think space will become a new travel destination? Why or why not?

PRE-LISTENING ACTIVITY 2

On the audio CD, you will hear people discussing space flights. Predict two things that you think they will say.

1. _____

2. _____

PRE-LISTENING VOCABULARY

A. You will hear a news story on the audio CD that includes the following words. Work with a partner or by yourself to find the definition of each word.

glitz	gala	aircraft	commercial	to fritter
to suspend	fuselage	bold	gamble	
atmosphere	to launch	gently	available	
view	to book			

Definitions	Vocabulary
1. very fancy, but superficial, flashiness; showiness associated with rich and famous people	glitz
2. brave; taking risks; not afraid of danger and very confident	
3. a very big party or celebration with special entertainment	
4. a bet; a risky action	
5. a machine which is able to fly	
6. the gases around the Earth (or another planet)	
7. for business or trade	
8. to send or shoot into the air or into water	
9. in a gentle or mild way, not in a rough way	
10. to waste for no good reason	
11. one can get it or use it	
12. to hang from somewhere	
13. something one can see or look at	
14. to buy a ticket or to reserve a place	
15. the main part or body of an aircraft	

B. Use the words from the list above to fill in the blanks in these sentences. Please make changes to verbs or nouns when necessary.

1. There was a __gala__ celebration after the company announced its future space flights.

2. Virgin Galactic has built a special _____ to take passengers into space.

3. The company hopes to make money on the _____ space flights.

4. Some people bought tickets on the space flights as soon as they were _____.

5. The company is taking a _____ that the space flights will be successful.

6. The owner of the company is not afraid of anything. He is a very _____ man.

7. The company will _____ the space flights from the spaceport in New Mexico.

8. The mother ship will take the spacecraft to the edge of the earth's _____.

9. Passengers think that the _____ of the earth from space will be incredible.

10. The spacecraft will float weightlessly for a while and then fall _____ towards the earth.

11. Hundreds of people have already _____ tickets on the first space flight.

12. The mother ship has two _____ and the spacecraft is _____ between them.

13. People who have the money to _____ away will probably take the flights into space.

Listening for the Main Ideas

Listen to the report and check off the correct answers to the questions.  **Track 81**

1. Where are the speakers?
   a. on radio/TV
   b. in Hollywood
   c. on a space flight

2. What kind of program is this?
   a. talk show
   b. news program
   c. travel show

3. How do the speakers feel about what they are discussing? Check all the adjectives that are correct.
   a. excited
   b. amazed
   c. enthusiastic
   d. frustrated

4. How many of your predictions in Pre-listening Activity 2 were correct? _____

Listening Comprehension

Track 82

Listening STRATEGY

If you check your guesses and predictions, this will help you keep track of your listening skills.

Listen to the report as many times as necessary. Write *T* if the statement is true or *F* if it is false.

1. The gala party was in Hollywood.   F

2. Billionaire businessman Richard Branson was at the celebration. _____

3. The commercial space flights will be cheap. _____

4. The space fights will last two and a half days. _____

5. The mother ship has the spaceship inside it. _____

6. Richard Branson thinks the aircraft isn't exciting. _____

7. The price of the ticket includes training before the flight. _____

8. The edge of space is over 1,000 kilometres above the earth. _____

9. Some people bought tickets on the space flight immediately. _____

10. The future passengers are excited because they will have an unforgettable view of the earth. _____

11. The flights will not start until the company has tested the aircraft more. _____

12. Richard Branson promises to start the space flights right away. _____

13. The Virgin Galactic company wants to prove that the aircraft is as safe as any aircraft that has gone into space before. _____

Personalizing

Work in a group of four. Discuss these questions:

Questions	Partner 1	Partner 2	Partner 3
What's the most unusual way you have travelled so far?			
What's the most expensive trip you have taken so far? Explain why you took this trip and why it was so expensive.			
What's the future of space flights, in your opinion?			
Would you like to take a flight into space? Explain why.			

Vocabulary and Language Chunks

Write the number of the expression next to the meaning. After checking your answers, choose five expressions and write your own sentences.

Words and Expressions

1. to fritter away
2. to roll out
3. to get you something
4. the edge of
5. to be done
6. so far
7. all at once
8. the rest of your life
9. more or less
10. at least

Meaning

___1___ to waste, not to use very well

_____ at the minimum

_____ approximately, about, nearly

_____ what remains of your life

_____ all at the same time

_____ to introduce a new product

_____ to buy you something

_____ to be finished

_____ up to this moment; until now

_____ the border; the boundary of; the limit of

SPEAKING ACTIVITY 13

Work with a partner. Ask each other these questions and report the three most interesting pieces of information to the class.

1. How many trips have you taken so far in your life? _____

    Where did you go? _____

2. How many wonders of the world have you seen so far? _____

    Which ones? _____

3. How many famous people have you seen so far? _____

    Who? _____

4. How many places have you lived in so far? _____

5. How many languages have you studied so far? _____

6. How many new friends have you met at this school so far? _____

7. How many jobs have you had so far? _____

8. How many movies have you seen so far this month? _____

    Which ones? _____

9. How many assignments have you done so far this month? _____

PRONUNCIATION

Pronunciation Focus 1: The Sound /æ/ as in *cat*

 **PRONUNCIATION ACTIVITY 1**

Track 83 Listen to these words with the / æ / sound. Repeat each word after you hear it.

class	bag	passport	travel	bank	map
plan	hat	last	happy	sad	man

PRONUNCIATION ACTIVITY 2

 Track 84 **A.** Listen to these sentences and underline the / æ / sound when you hear it. Check your answers with the class.

1. Can I see your passport?

2. Please put your bag at the back.

3. She's happy because she's been travelling a lot.

4. The man with the map is very sad.

5. Do they plan to go to the bank?

6. He's happy because he isn't last in his class.

7. She bought a new hat at last.

8. You can't take your cat on the plane.

9. They wanted to see exotic animals in Africa.

B. Work with a partner and practise saying the sentences.

C. Write down three words with the / æ / sound that you use often. Make sentences with these words and practise saying them to your partner.

PRONUNCIATION ACTIVITY 3

A. Listen to these words. Write each word in the correct column according to the vowel sound in the word.

Track 85

Words with the sound /æ/	Words with the sound /a/
hat	hot

B. Check your answers and then make up four sentences using as many of these words as you can. Work with a partner and practise saying these sentences.

_____

_____

_____

Pronunciation Focus 2: Contrasting the Sound /ɛ/ as in *get* and /ey/ as in *gate*

PRONUNCIATION ACTIVITY 4

A. Listen to these words with the / ɛ / sound. Repeat each word after you hear it.

 Track 86

get	met	left	better	send	sell	any
end	enter	test	let	never	explore	exam
temperate	bear	exit	guess	help	edge	fell

B. Choose three words with the sound / ɛ / which you use a lot. Write sentences with these words and work with a partner to practise saying them.

PRONUNCIATION ACTIVITY 5

Track 87

A. Listen to these words with the / ey / sound. Repeat each word after you hear it.

main	plate	gate	taste	late	mate	hail
date	paper	age	hate	great	say	rain

B. Choose three words with the sound / ey / which you use a lot. Write sentences with these words and work with a partner to practise saying them.

_____

_____

_____

PRONUNCIATION ACTIVITY 6

Track 88

A. Listen to these pairs of words. Circle *same* or *different* for each pair.

1. same   (different)   8. same   different
2. (same)   different   9. same   different
3. same   different   10. same   different
4. same   different   11. same   different
5. same   different   12. same   different
6. same   different   13. same   different
7. same   different

B. Work with a partner and make up your own sentences using five of the words. Practise saying the sentences to each other.

PRONUNCIATION ACTIVITY 7

Track 89

A. Listen to the sentences. After you hear each sentence, write it down.

1. _____
2. _____
3. _____
4. _____
5. _____
6. _____

B. Check your answers with the class and work with a partner to practise saying the sentences.

COMMUNICATING IN THE REAL WORLD

A. Use your English to talk to people outside your classroom. On your own or with a partner, talk to five people outside your class. Ask them the questions below and record the information. Make a short report to the class about what you learned.

Before you begin, say this:

> May I ask you some questions? This is an assignment for my English class.

1. What famous places have you visited?

2. What place would you like to visit? Why?

3. Would you like to take a flight into space when these are available?

4. What places in this country or province should people call wonders of the world?

5. How long have you been living in this city?

6. In your opinion, what's the most interesting neighbourhood?

7. What are the best things about this city?

B. Project: Work with one or two partners and choose a neighbourhood in this city. Take some pictures of the most interesting or most important parts of it. Do some research about the neighbourhood. Find out about the people, history, homes, lifestyle, recreation, and transportation in the area. Then make a poster or PowerPoint presentation about the neighbourhood. Be prepared to answer questions.

SELF-EVALUATION

Think about your work in this chapter. For each row in the chart sections Grammar and Language Functions, Learning Strategies, and Pronunciation, give yourself a score based on the rating scale below and write a comment in the Notes section.

Show the chart to your teacher. Talk about what you need to do to make your English better.

Rating Scale

1	2	3	4	5

Needs improvement. ←————————————————————————————→ Great!

	Score	Notes
Grammar and Language Functions		
talking about travelling and cultural differences		
talking and asking about experiences and accomplishments in the indefinite past		
asking questions and making statements with the present perfect and adverbs of frequency		
asking for and giving information about actions begun in the past and continuing to the present		
using the superlative degree of adjectives		
Pronunciation		
recognizing and pronouncing the vowels /a/ and /æ/		
recognizing and pronouncing the vowels /ey/ and /ɛ/		
Learning Strategies		
Speaking		
using social strategies such as asking questions to extend conversations and get more practice in making conversation		
Listening		
listening for similarities in place names in my first language and English to help me understand		
checking my guesses and predictions in listening to keep track of my listening skills		

Vocabulary and Language Chunks

Look at this list of new vocabulary and language chunks you learned in this chapter. Give yourself a score based on the rating scale and write a comment.

to get hooked on	to get through	lifestyle
to roll out	backpack	to step up
to grow up	to fritter away	to take a toll
a couple of	all at once	to get you
to stand out	all over the place	the edge of
to be done	to attract a crowd	see the sights
the rest of your life	so far	more or less
at least		

	Score	Notes
understanding new vocabulary and language chunks		
using new words and phrases correctly		

Write six sentences and use new vocabulary you learned in this chapter.

1. _____

2. _____

3. _____

4. _____

5. _____

6. _____

My plan for practising is _____

_____

_____

_____

_____

APPENDIX

Irregular Verbs

A. These irregular verbs don't follow a specific rule in forming the simple past and past participle. The forms need to be memorized.

Base Form	Simple Past	Past Participle
be	was, were	been
beat	beat	beaten
bite	bit	bitten
break	broke	broken
choose	chose	chosen
do	did	done
fly	flew	flown
forget	forgot	forgotten
freeze	froze	frozen
get	got	got (gotten)
go	went	gone
lie	lay	lain
read	read	read
ride	rode	ridden
speak	spoke	spoken
steal	stole	stolen
tear	tore	torn
write	wrote	written
wake	woke	woken

B. The following five types of irregular verbs follow specific patterns in forming the past and the past participle.

Group 1

All three verb forms are the same.

Base Form	Simple Past	Past Participle
bet	bet	bet
cost	cost	cost
cut	cut	cut
fit	fit	fit
hit	hit	hit
hurt	hurt	hurt
let	let	let
put	put	put
quit	quit	quit
shut	shut	shut
spread	spread	spread

Group 2

In these verbs, the form for the past and the past participle is the same.

Base Form	Simple Past	Past Participle
bring	brought	brought
build	built	built
buy	bought	bought
catch	caught	caught
feed	fed	fed
feel	felt	felt
fight	fought	fought
find	found	found
hang	hung	hung
have	had	had
hear	heard	heard
hold	held	held
keep	kept	kept
kneel	knelt	knelt
lay	laid	laid
lead	led	led
leave	left	left
lend	lent	lent
lose	lost	lost
make	made	made
mean	meant	meant
meet	met	met
pay	paid	paid
say	said	said
sell	sold	sold
send	sent	sent
shine	shone	shone
shoot	shot	shot
sit	sat	sat
sleep	slept	slept
spend	spent	spent
stand	stood	stood
strike	struck	struck
teach	taught	taught
tell	told	told
think	thought	thought
understand	understood	understood

Group 3

In these verbs, the vowels change from *i* in the present to *a* in the past and *u* in the past participle.

Base Form	Simple Past	Past Participle
begin	began	begun
drink	drank	drunk
ring	rang	rung
shrink	shrank	shrunk
sing	sang	sung
sink	sank	sunk
swim	swam	swum

Group 4

In these verbs, the past participle is the same as the base form, but we add -*n* or -*en* to the past participle.

Base Form	Simple Past	Past Participle
blow	blew	blown
draw	drew	drawn
drive	drove	driven
eat	ate	eaten
fall	fell	fallen
give	gave	given
grow	grew	grown
hide	hid	hidden
know	knew	known
shake	shook	shaken
take	took	taken
throw	threw	thrown

Group 5

In these verbs, the past participle is the same as the base form of the verb.

Base Form	Simple Past	Past Participle
become	became	become
come	came	come
run	ran	run

CREDITS

Photo and Figure Credits